UNCAGED

UNCAGED

Released to Live in the Freedom of God's Promises

JUD WILHITE

fedd books

ISBN: 978-1-943217-81-6

eISBN: 978-1-943217-82-3

To Emma and Ethan

CONTENTS

INTRODUCTION

WHY I HAD TO WRITE THIS BOOK....9

1. PRESENCE IS THE PROMISE....15

2. LITTLE BLUE BOXES AND STAIRWAYS TO HEAVEN....41

3. A BREATH OF FRESH AIR....63

4. BOOMERANG YOUR BLESSINGS....83

5. A NEW MIXTAPE....103

6. THE FORBIDDEN RED VELVET CUPCAKE....123

7. PLAN Z....145

8. WEAVER OF DREAMS....163

CONCLUSION

ON WINGS LIKE EAGLES....185

ACKNOWLEDGEMENTS....189

ABOUT THE AUTHOR....191

NOTES....193

INTRODUCTION

WHY I HAD TO WRITE THIS BOOK

Years ago, I had the biggest interview of my life. NBC's *Today* came to Las Vegas and filmed a major segment on our church to air on the show. They interviewed me and my wife, Lori, and others from Central Church, highlighting the work we were doing for people. Their angle was on a young pastor (me) in a crazy city (Vegas) leading a movement of compassion for others that was spreading like wildfire. We were thrilled and thought this was a great way to emphasize some of the awesome work our church was doing.

A short time later, the airdate was set and I announced it to the whole church. On that morning when it was supposed to air, tornadoes hit in the Midwest, and they covered those stories and postponed ours. The next airdate was postponed by breaking news, as well. As was the next. And the biggest interview I ever did . . . never aired. It sits as some digital file on a network hard drive, an orphan in cyberspace.

I'm the guy interviewed by the *Today* show whose interview never actually aired.

DO HIS PROMISES MATTER?

To this day, that whole incident remains a head-scratcher. I don't know why a major network would send out a crew, film it, invest money, and then never show it. And to top it off, the primary reason our segment was bumped resulted from what insurers would call an "act of God"—tornadoes. What in the world was God up to?

I still don't have answers, but these questions lead to other, more troubling, questions, unanswerable ones much more frustrating and painful than why our taped segment wasn't broadcast on a TV show. Questions like:

What can I really expect from God?

Why do I seem to take one step forward and two steps back in my spiritual life?

Why do I get so disappointed when my experience doesn't match up with my expectations about what God's doing in my life?

What has he really promised you and me on which we can completely anchor our lives?

What difference do God's promises make when hard things happen—crazy hard things like cancer and unemployment, adultery and divorce, addictions and car accidents?

As a pastor, I'm often confronted with these questions from people struggling to make sense of their lives in the midst of devastating circumstances. In fact, near misses and what-ifs often feel like the story of life, and sometimes we have no idea why something did or didn't happen. But what I've learned over the years is that, most of the time, people don't expect specific, logical answers as much as they long to be heard. They seek assurance that no matter what they're facing, their faith still counts. Their relationship with God still matters, and his promises to them are still true despite their feelings to the contrary.

During a recent season of near burnout, I began reflecting on God's promises and being honest about whether they make a real difference in my life. To begin with, I wasn't sure I could even name all the actual promises found in God's Word to his people. So many pat answers and bumper-sticker clichés float around about God that I began to wonder which ones are actually in the Bible and which ones are just popular slogans to make us feel better. Other than forgiveness for our sins and eternal life, strength when you need it, and help in times of trouble, I couldn't go into great detail about what else God actually promises us.

Those are no small items to be sure, but they still feel general and vague—theological answers floating on clouds out there somewhere. Not a great place to go when, as a pastor, I'm daily trying to offer real hope to others. So I began looking for books on God's promises because, after all, what can we really hope to receive from God other than what he has promised? I found most of them to be a list of different Bible passages—a good place to begin but only scratching the surface of what I was after.

The more I kept digging, however, the more disappointed I became. My search eventually led to a year of my own devotional study on God's promises. I filled up pages and pages of notes on what God's promises were and what they meant. Again and again, I was challenged about some of my false assumptions of what God promised to do versus what I wanted him to do. I was troubled to see how much of my view of life and faith was anchored in my presumptions about what God would do for me rather than in his actual promises.

Sure, I know the Bible teaches that life will be hard, that things don't always make sense, and that disappointments will be plenty, *and* that God still cares, still loves us, and is still at work, nevertheless. While I understand we're living in between heaven and earth, in between what is seen and unseen, in between circumstantial evidence and eternal reality, I'm not sure I fully appreciated what it means to live in this tension. If I did, I wouldn't be surprised when crazy things happened.

But the more I pressed in, the more I understood and absorbed his promises. They began to balance out my expectations, both lifting them in some ways and tempering them in others. Each day, I faced a choice to really trust in his promises and live in the freedom I have through my relationship with Jesus. To build my life on them. To take God at his Word and believe he would show up according to what he's promised. To know the difference between what's true and what's just wishful thinking. To live by faith and love by choice. To trust the goodness of God even in a world that's not.

Eventually, joy and gratitude began flooding my heart from the wellspring of God's promises, and I began to start writing about them. As God's promises grew in my heart, I just couldn't keep them to myself. I had to write this book! Corny as that may sound, it's true. At the very least, I know the difference focusing on God's promises has made and continues to make in my life, and I want the same for you.

So what you have in front of you is the way eight promises of God have reframed my life. Initially, I started writing it for myself, to get the promises of God deeper into my own heart and leave a legacy for my kids. Now I'm thrilled to share what I've learned with you in hopes to pass along the catalyst for one of the most significant shifts in my faith. There's nothing magical about these eight promises, and they're certainly not just steps for an easier life. But I'm convinced they can help you rethink the way you see God, your relationship with him, and consequently how you live your life.

You have been set free.

You can leave your cage of circumstances and walk by faith.

You can walk in freedom every day.

You can live *uncaged*!

CHAPTER 1

PRESENCE IS THE PROMISE

Recently, I read about an incident at the Los Angeles Zoo. An employee named Gary Richmond noticed a cage full of fifteen red-tailed hawks kept in a back room, leftover evidence in a defunct poaching case. They could not be displayed and would likely die in captivity. So, being a rebel at heart, Richmond decided to "accidentally" leave their cage door open and give them a chance to escape back into the wild.

Returning an hour later, he was shocked to see all the hawks were still there. So then he charged at them like a bear, trying to scare them out. Most of them flew a few feet away but looked back longingly at the cage that had become their home. Richmond couldn't believe what he was seeing and shouted: "Don't you see the sky? That's what you're meant for. . . You're not chickens. You are majestic birds of prey. . . God gave you a purpose, now go fulfill it."[1]

None of them budged, and he eventually herded them

back into their cage. The hawks got so used to a caged life that they forgot what it meant to be free. They traded predictability for purpose, bravery for boredom, the empty promise of the cage for the unlimited promise of freedom.

It's the same trade we make every day.

We forget that Jesus didn't just die to save us *from* our sins—he died to save us *to* a brand-new life; a life free from worry, fear, shame, and condemnation; a life where God's power and promises live in us and work through us in all things; a life where we are finally free to stop pursuing things that don't satisfy and start pursuing our God-given purpose with God-given bravery. True freedom isn't doing whatever we want; it's becoming who God made us to be. God charges at our cage saying, "Fly! Be free! Be who I created you to be!" But, too often, we settle for life in the cage instead.

The amazing news is that the cage remains *unlocked*. You're already free through faith in Christ! The trick is living in this freedom, understanding and believing that God's promises can teach you to fly again. And that's what this book is all about. Like the man at the zoo, I hope to point out the open door in front of you and call you to more. Understanding the power of God's promises, you'll see how to cling to God's presence when you're overwhelmed, boldly tap into God's blessing for your need, step out of condemnation into liberation, rely on God's Spirit when you're weak, and walk in God's power when you're tempted.

You will understand why Peter calls them "great and precious promises," which "enable you to share his divine nature and escape the world's corruption caused by human desires" (2 Peter 1:4). The term "enable" means "to strengthen." God's promises *empower* you. They give you the strength to face what you can't face on your own. They help you to face the world in all of its challenges with faith and hope that are mature and grounded. They fill you with courage and lead you to freedom. They provide peace and comfort that transcend anything rational or logical.

George Macdonald once said that people never tire of life, but they tire of death.[2] He means that when you're overwhelmed or underwhelmed, the problem isn't too much of life coming at you. The problem is too little of God's life flowing through you. You don't have the inner power to meet the outer challenges. This power, this life, is something that flows out of the promises we hold dear. When God's promises are forgotten or abandoned, the flow of life stops. When his promises are remembered and activated, he strengthens you. He gives you what you need; what you cannot give yourself. The great I AM makes sure that you *are*, you *will* and you *can*.

Jesus declared that he came to give his people life to the fullest. You walk into that full life by walking in the promises of God. They are the bedrock of not just the Christian life, but of all life. When you connect to his promises, you reconnect to your source of life and your life overflows. Love, joy, and peace well up within you and spill out for others. Faith comes alive as you trust God to do what you cannot do yourself. Hope becomes more solid, real, and clear as you rely on him to show up in specific ways. You live in the holy tension between being underwhelmed by what you can do, and overjoyed by what God's promises can do.

His promises are the path to everything God will do for you and through you. They are everything you can expect from the One who loves you most.

This is your opportunity to be free.

God is calling you.

It's time to leave your cage.

OPEN DOORS

Part of the problem of living in the freedom of God's promises comes from our uncertainty about what to do with such liberty. Tending toward the extremes, we often either ignore the open door—or even try to lock it again ourselves—or attempt to bust down doors in areas where life isn't working the way we want it to. These extremes remind me of a little incident at home recently.

Walking in the door after work, I knew right away there was a huge problem. Tension hung in the air like a fine mist, invisible, but tangible nonetheless. My wife Lori, usually calm and composed, looked at me with her jaws clenched and eyes blazing.

"*I'm done*!" she said, firing her words with the intensity of a Taser. "Two doors are off their hinges—*two*!"

I wasn't sure what she meant but knew it wasn't good.

Our household stress was already high. It was the last week of school before summer break. Both our kids had finals. After months of carpooling, juggling extracurriculars, checking grades, and homework-nagging, we were all exhausted. And Lori, an amazing teacher and our in-house educational ninja, had spent the past four nights working with our kids to prepare them for their upcoming exams. But that evening, our son Ethan had hit a wall. Like an overloaded laptop, he shut down and refused any more test prep. In a final act of non-cooperation, he stood up, walked to his room, and locked himself in.

To appreciate the severity of this scene, you must understand that both Lori and Ethan are the easygoing peacemakers in our house. Lori especially provides an even-keeled force for good. At first, this situation was no different. She repeatedly knocked on Ethan's door and tried to reason with him. No response. She calmly threatened to take privileges away. No response. She then decided to unlock the door herself but couldn't find the weird little key that fits through the hole in the doorknob.

Exasperated, she warned him: "If you don't open this door *right now* I'm taking it off its hinges!" Silence. He was calling her bluff, but she was not joking. While Lori stormed off to grab a screwdriver, Ethan, acting in both fear and defiance, retreated to the room next to his and locked that door, too.

Lori returned and got down to business. Fueled by adrenaline, she unscrewed all twelve screws by hand in record time. Meanwhile, Ethan peeked out to see the horror of his bedroom door off its hinges. He knew there was no place to hide as Lori attacked the second door, which was now open!

Listening to her breathless narrative, I didn't have the

heart to tell her it's much easier to tap out the hinge pins than unscrew all the hinges. I didn't have the heart, and I'm not a complete idiot.

A few hours later, Ethan apologized and they hugged it out, but he didn't get his doors back in place until after finals week. Stacked against the wall of our bedroom, the two unhinged doors leaned there like a metaphor for life. Sometimes we feel overwhelmed and tilt toward the extremes. We want to bolt the doors and hide, refusing to embrace the freedom on the other side, or we break down the doors blocking our path, determined to make life work on our terms. And either way, the doors aren't the only things to come unhinged.

AGAINST THE ODDS

When life spins out of control and we feel overwhelmed, it's hard to believe that we might be exactly where God wants us to be. But as you read through the Bible, you see a disturbing pattern. God often leads his people into places where they feel overwhelmed. The task is too large. The enemies too strong. The threats too big. The odds too great. The escapes unbearably narrow. The rescues virtually impossible. The eventual, redemptive outcomes unimaginable.

Abraham, Isaac, and Jacob struggled to hang on to God's promises in the face of numerous obstacles, both internal and external. Moses stood before the burning bush and pleaded for God to send someone else. Joshua paused at the prospect of leading a million ex-slaves into the promised land, something his mentor Moses could not do. Gideon was told to conquer an enemy with a shockingly small and shrinking army. Jeremiah, Ezekiel, and Haggai were told to speak cutting truths to calloused hearts. Ruth left her homeland, widowed and afraid, to follow her bitter, impoverished mother-in-law. Rahab harbored foreign spies, leaving her life and the safety of her family hanging by a scarlet thread.

Even after Jesus arrived on the scene, this pattern continued. Proclaiming himself to be the long-anticipated Messiah, Jesus was often rejected by the Jewish people. His scared disciples then watched their master die in the most excruciating and humiliating way possible, nailed to a cross like a common criminal. Even after Christ's resurrection, his dazed disciples watched him rise through the clouds and wondered what was next. After a dramatic midlife U-turn, the apostle Paul was consistently battered, blocked, and burdened as he struggled to take the good news of Jesus to the world.

In all these cases where people felt overwhelmed and life felt unhinged, one promise was given, and it was given by God himself: *I'll be with you*. It was not a promise of comfort, convenience, or construction. It was a promise of presence. God consistently promised to walk with his people through their overwhelming scenarios.

And even as life often felt unhinged or situations looked hopeless, God was not restrained by what held them back. Sometimes he opened a door. Sometimes he blew the door off its hinges. Sometimes he held them safely in the shelter of his wings. Sometimes he provided what they needed. And always, God met them where they were and did what appeared to be impossible. And in every case, they did more, went farther and had a greater impact than human effort alone can achieve.

It's a powerful promise to know that God is still with us today. This promise of God's presence can lead you from overwhelmed to overflowing. You won't necessarily escape your burden, but you will be empowered to bear up within the fight until God brings victory. When you are struggling, feeling alone and isolated, when you can't see God moving and working in your life, this is the promise you are tempted to forget. You face seasons where your plan doesn't pan out and the blows keep coming. You lose perspective. You get overwhelmed. In these seasons, in every season, you need the promise of God's presence.

No wonder this promise is mentioned more than all the others. In fact, the greatest promise of God in the Bible is not his blessing, help, or even rewards. The greatest promise is God himself. His presence *is* the promise, a shelter in the crazy storms of life. You and I aren't promised a life without hardships or difficulties. "In this world you will have trouble" Jesus said, "But take heart! I have overcome the world" (John 16:33, NIV). As a believer, we may face the same tragedies and heartaches as anyone else, but the promise of God's presence makes an enormous difference—an eternal difference as well as an immediate one.

MIC DROP MOMENT

Before you dismiss what I'm saying as the same old spiritual spiel you've heard before, stay with me because I used to feel the same way. You may have heard this promise before, but owning it in your heart has *huge* benefits. And living in its freedom reminds us to walk out of the cage of circumstances—toward that which is eternal—every time.

Before I became a follower of Jesus, I believed God's big purpose was to keep me in line and inspire me to be good. Neither sounded like much fun, so I wasn't very interested. Later, after coming to faith, it seemed like forgiveness and eternal life were the point. I could be forgiven for my sins, and I could live forever. Who wouldn't want that, right? But as I grew in my faith, I saw that these were all a means to an end. Forgiveness was how a deep relationship with God was possible. Eternal life was the span in which this relationship was enjoyed. The *relationship*, the presence of God in my life, was what mattered most.

We read in the opening pages of Genesis that God was present, "walking" with Adam and Eve in the garden of Eden. The description is one of paradise and intimacy. Adam and Eve were to multiply and have dominion over the earth. They were to fill the earth, ultimately spreading God's relational presence across the earth through their family. Sin broke that relational connection, and the story going forward is about God re-establishing his presence in our lives.

From the call of Abraham to the covenants with Israel, God's presence with his people was the aim. From the tabernacle to the temple, providing a place for his presence was the goal. From Jesus who is called Immanuel, meaning "God with us," to the church community as the hands and feet of Christ—the new temple of his Spirit—God's presence remains our miracle. This miracle explains why the overarching story of the Bible is called the "Immanuel principle"—because the big theme boils down to God with us. And the really good news is that his presence remains with us because of his faithfulness more than our own—so when we blow it, God never abandons us.

We see this assurance revealed in the last chapters of Revelation with its epic depiction of the end goal of all God's work: a new world God creates for the faithful, his heaven colliding with our earth. Notice how John describes this beautiful, majestic scene: "I heard a loud shout from the throne, saying, 'Look, God's home is now among his people! He will live with them, and they will be his people. *God himself will be with them.* He will wipe every tear from their eyes, and there will be no more death or sorrow or crying or pain. All these things are gone forever'" (Revelation 21:3–4, emphasis added).

This new creation boasts more than the promise of no more suffering or even the promise of heaven, as we often imagine it. This eternity is the highest promise of heaven, God himself. This is Eden recaptured and recreated, God walking with his people in profound intimacy again. Both Eden and the new creation contain similar elements like the tree of life. Yet, in the new creation there is no mention of walls or gates between you and God. There are no separate areas like the temple had with the Holy Place and Most Holy Place. There is no sin getting in the way. The image of what's coming is God's presence freely and fully with us as his people. What makes heaven perfect is the ultimate goodness, truth, and beauty of God's presence without veil or limit.

This is the ultimate mic drop moment: "God himself will be with them" (Revelation 21:3).

This is where your heart erupts with joy and unimaginable relief. The entire Bible, all the twists and turns of God's interaction with people, lead to this. The crucifixion, resurrection, and ascension of Jesus ensure this. The church, in all its dysfunction and beauty, proclaims this. Everything points to this. All the other promises of God are fully fulfilled here—*God himself will be with them.*

This scripture illustrates the whole shebang in a sentence, the big idea in a nutshell. And here's the awesome part: this promise is more than a future hope—*it's the present reality as you walk with God by faith.* You get to relate with the One who is everything today! And you will experience him even more fully in heaven tomorrow. This promise drives all others, for God is the ultimate reward—a taste of pure heaven for your heart while here on earth.

NAUGHTY OR NICE

If you struggle to get excited about this promise, it likely stems from your misperception of God and his character. If you're like me, you need to strip away your false impressions about God in order to experience the full freedom that comes with his presence. My early perception of God was similar to the song, "Santa Claus is Coming to Town." He's not only checking his list to see how good you have been, but he's watching you sleep. Seriously, does it not seem strange that Santa watches you when you're sleeping?

Yikes. A creeper *and* he's judgmental. Not someone's presence you want 24/7!

Thankfully, God is not Santa. The point of his presence isn't just to keep you in line and give you toys. He strengthens and helps, comforts and consoles—he is in a dedicated relationship with you. We see this again and again throughout scripture, and while the promise, "I am with you," occurs in many places in the Bible, I repeatedly return to one favorite passage for strength and comfort: "Don't be afraid, for I am with you. Don't be discouraged, for I am your God. I will strengthen you and help you. I will hold you up with my victorious right hand" (Isaiah 41:10).

When I face fear and discouragement, weakness and need, this promise echoes in my mind and heart. I love it because God isn't just saying he *can* help me, but he *will.* Because I don't need possibilities in my moment of trial: I need real-time rescue. I don't need more platitudes and clichés; I need presence and strength. I don't need somebody's good intentions; I need to be lifted up by God's "victorious right hand," which is exactly what God says he will do.

John Piper teases out the promise of Isaiah 41:10 by noting the five prepositions that relate to both God and you:

"I am your God..." — God is *over you.*

"I am with you..." — God is *by you.*

"I will strengthen you..." — God is *in you.*

"I will help you..." — God is *around you.*

"I will hold you up..."— God is *underneath you.* [3]

This is the God who is not simply there, but *there for you.* Because his presence to help is over, by, inside, around, and underneath you, your temporary fear and discouragement lose their power. Instead, courage and strength flow into you even when it feels like life's coming off the hinges. Still don't believe me? Then let's unpack each of these prepositions—*over, by, in, around, underneath*—to see more clearly the depth of his promise to be present with us.

OVER YOU

God's presence with you includes his presence over you as God. He is sovereign in strength and power. He is completely unrivaled. He's the ultimate loving, protective Father. The most artistic, inspired Creator. He is unrivaled and incomparable, which often makes it hard for us to get a handle on experiencing his actual presence.

I'm reminded of a while back when Lori came out of the bedroom wearing a new dress. It was loose-fitting, black and white, and flowed down to her ankles. She said, "Do I look okay in this dress?" Technically, it wasn't a question. She wanted affirmation that she was beautiful and looked good in anything—which is true.

I said, "You look like a whale."

In that millisecond, as the words hung in the air, I

thought, "Have you lost your mind? You idiot! What are you doing?"

The confused, hurt look on Lori's face said it all.

I quickly spun into damage control: "I don't mean that the way it sounded! I'm not saying you are big like a whale. I mean that the dress is black and white, and reminds me of Sea World, and the whales there are black and white, you know?" Every word dug me further into a hole.

Fortunately, we've been married for over twenty years, so Lori knows my heart. She knows I think she's beautiful, and I tell her often. She also knows that sometimes I speak before I think. She looked at me, put her hand up, and said, "You need to stop now."

I was only making it worse.

By the grace of God, she accepted my apology and dropped it.

My wife expected an affirmation that she looked good in the dress—or in anything—which was correct. I understood the situation, but in the moment, I didn't respond well. Her question wasn't seeking an answer, and I was foolish to give her one, especially one that referred to a mammal measured in tons.

God asks a different question, but he also doesn't seek an answer: "'To whom will you compare me? Who is my equal?' asks the Holy One" (Isaiah 40:25). This appears as a question, but God's actually making a statement: he's beyond equal. There's *nothing* to compare him to that accurately expresses his power, goodness, mercy, and love.

In making this kind of bold reminder, he's raising his

hand to your fear, worry, and lack of faith and saying, "You need to stop now." The questions end here. The sentence concludes with, "asks the Holy One." Holy means set apart. God is totally set apart, unique, distinct, sacred, and incomparable. This verse might be roughly translated: "'Who is like me?' asks the One whom no one is like."

After implying that nothing compares to him, God draws a limited association—the star-filled sky. He says, "Look up into the heavens. Who created all the stars? He brings them out like an army, one after another, calling each by its name. Because of his great power and incomparable strength, not a single one is missing" (40:26).

Let's think about this. According to experts, there are at least seventy sextillion stars in the universe.[4] This number represents a seven with twenty-two zeros after it, which isn't very helpful to someone like me, who flunked Algebra II. To put the number into perspective, that's ten times the grains of sand on all the world's beaches *and* deserts. That's a lot of stars and there are likely more.

But God remembers each one and calls them out by name. In the ancient world, to know the name of something was to know its essence and thus to have power over it. Calling the stars by name reinforces that God is all-knowing and all-powerful, sovereign over deep space, stars, galaxies, moons, planets, asteroids, magnetic fields, and cosmic rays.

In times of discouragement and fear, walk outside and look up. The stars can't rival God, but they show off his vastness and provide scale for our smallness. I remember sitting on an isolated beach on the North Shore of Hawaii late at night. Staring up at the dark glittering sky, I listened to the powerful waves crash as the tide rolled in, alone but for the stars—thousands of them so far above me. Along with the immense and unsettling power of millions of gallons of water crashing just beyond my feet, I felt small and vulnerable, a speck on the edge of the world.

Sitting on that dark beach, I started to pray, filled with wonder at the One who knows the essence of each star. He is large and in charge, working when I can't see it. He rules the heavens and earth, the animals and elements, the fish of the sea and birds of the air. He holds back the waters and calls forth the stars. My problems withered in the face of such power and might. My worries shrunk before such raw and total control. By the time I rose, I no longer felt alone or helpless, but empowered and loved by a God who is beyond compare.

When all you see are your circumstances, discouragement blindsides you. But when you look up and consider God in his strength, you remember that he towers over your circumstances. God is bigger than your mortgage, overdue bills, or credit card debt—bigger than your report card, rap sheet, broken engagement, or secret addiction. He is larger than your loneliness, faithful in your frustration, present in your pressure. He comforts in pain, gives patience in the craziness, shows mercy in failure.

No matter how big your problems seem, God is bigger.

Look up to the sky tonight and consider the stars.

Remind yourself, and your problems, how big your God is.

BY YOU

God is not only present over you as sovereign ruler, he is also present *by your side* to calm your fear. No wonder that he frequently tells us to not be afraid. Jesus gives no less than 125 command statements in the Gospels, but the one he issues most—twenty-one times—deals with the theme of fear. These include statements like "do not be afraid," "fear not," "have courage," or "take heart." To put that in perspective, the command theme to love God and your neighbor appears only eight times. As far as quantity goes, the command Jesus issues more than any other is *fear not.*[5]

Jesus doesn't issue this command to convince us that there's nothing to be afraid of. He's well aware there's plenty for us to fear. But he's reminding us that we can rely on his presence in the face of fear, similar to what David writes, "Even when I walk through the darkest valley, I will not be afraid, for you are close beside me" (Psalm 23:4). The darkest valley, or shadow of death as the King James translates it, could literally read, "the shadowest of shadows."

David never assumes that because he loves God, he won't face fearful things. He still walks through that dark valley. Nowhere in the Bible do you see believers engage in the magical thinking that God's love transforms trials into unicorns and lollipops. David, like countless others then and now, walks through the shadows but won't succumb to fear because God was by him, beside him, all the way.

If you aren't in the shadowest of shadows right now, you probably have been or will be. Your health fails or your kids get bullied. A family member betrays you or past mistakes come back to threaten your future, or maybe on the surface everything looks okay, but you're still hurting inside. You wonder where the desire went to wake up in the morning and dive into the day. Shadows creep in, the will to fight fades, and you don't know why.

During these dark times, remember that it's part of our normal human experience to face different valleys, narrows, and ravines. David's comfort isn't that God will remove the valleys, but that he is present in them. God is by you in the crisis, the health concern, the depression. He is by you in your family drama or work stress. He is by you in the financial downturn.

If you're tempted to think God doesn't care about where you are right now, think back. When life appears dark, don't forget all God has done for you in the light. In the shadow of the valley, remember the joy you once felt and the satisfaction you once knew. You will get there again because the same God is beside you. David knew he'd get there again. He ends the Psalm saying, "Surely your goodness and unfailing love will pursue me all the days of my life, and I will live in the house of the LORD forever" (Psalm 23:6). Even in the darkest of shadows, David knew God's goodness and love literally tracked him down. No matter what came in this life, he would dwell with God forever. God was the great One beside him, his presence guiding and protecting.

God is beside you.

Don't give in to fear.

IN YOU

God's presence with you means that he is not only over you and by you, but he is also *in you* through his Spirit. He strengthens you from the inside out. Paul prayed that you would understand God's "incomparably great power for us who believe. That power is the same as the mighty strength, he exerted when he raised in Christ from the dead and seated him at his right hand in the heavenly realms" (Ephesians 1:19–20, NIV).

Four words are used here to describe this force of God for your good. The first word is "power," a term from which we get the word dynamite, God's explosive power. Next, he writes of God's "exertion," and then "might," referring to God's "mighty strength." All four words—power, exertion, might, and strength—refer to God's work in you. Paul doesn't pray you will get this power. He prays you will realize *you already have it*. Through faith you can access God's incredible power—the same power that raised Christ from the dead.

I admit this sounds amazing, but in my own experience it feels hard to comprehend. Too often I am weak and tired. I believe this inner power is available to me, but I struggle to get past my feelings and engage my faith. A young kid at church calls me, "Pastor Superman," which is funny when I think of how un-super I often feel, a far cry from leaping tall buildings in a single bound.

Often, the power Paul talks about is taken to mean something it was never meant to mean. Paul's life gives us clues about what this power really looks like. He writes, "We now have this light shining in our hearts, but we ourselves are like fragile clay jars containing this great treasure. *This makes it clear that our great power is from God, not from ourselves*" (2 Corinthians 4:7, emphasis added). God's light shines into our hearts, but we're like old pottery. We are weak and frail and riddled with holes. We're broken at best, full of rough edges, thin places, cracks, and crevices. Our weakness makes it crystal clear that our power is from God. Paul then admits he is "pressed on every side by troubles" (4:8). This doesn't sound like Superman or Mr. Incredible.

You might assume that if God's power is in you, then you shouldn't feel so much pressure. Yet pressure is what you likely feel every day—life, family, and emotional pressure. (If you want to feel some right now, just balance your checkbook.) Sometimes you can be tempted to think, "Maybe it's just me, I'm doing something wrong and not able to access God's power." Yet Paul was an incredibly devout person, arguably the greatest missionary the church has ever produced, and was pressed by troubles everywhere.

God's power doesn't dissolve the pressure, but refines your faith through the pressure. Paul says the difference God's power makes is simply, "we are not crushed" (4:8). He gives you the ability to endure and to persevere, to feel the weight of your troubles, but to not be crushed by them. Life's pressure cooker produces a more perfected faith.

Paul continues, "We are perplexed" (4:8). If life is anything, it is perplexing. Why am I not experiencing more peace at home? Why do I keep making the same bad decisions? How is Rolling Stones guitarist, Keith Richards, still alive after all his partying while I'm hitting the gym and falling apart?

Surely if you were in touch with God's power, this confusion would lift. Yet, for Paul the confusion doesn't lift, but God's power in him means he is "not driven to despair" (4:8). God empowers you to press on when it's perplexing. You may want to despair, but you're enabled to keep moving forward.

Paul says, "We get knocked down but we are not destroyed" (4:9). God's power doesn't make you a boxer like Floyd Mayweather. You may hit the canvas repeatedly, but God strengthens you to keep getting up. The measure of a person is never how many times you are knocked down, but how many times you get back up.

All of this can reframe your perspective on God's presence and power in you. This power doesn't make you super-human but gives you the ability to push through incredible odds. If you're pressed, perplexed, or knocked down, this just means you're human. God in you means these struggles don't define you; they deepen your dependence.

AROUND YOU

God's presence with you is also his presence *around you.* He covers your rear guard and watches your back. He goes before you and makes a way. He's a 360-degree God.

This covering is significant no matter how you tend to approach life. From my experience, there are generally two types of people: planners and wingers. Planners love to plan it all out while wingers love to wing it. In my marriage, I'm the planner and Lori is the winger. I'm great with being spontaneous, I just want to plan it—you know, starting at 5:00 p.m. we're going to be spontaneous until 9:00 p.m. I try to explain to Lori that I always have a working plan. If we don't plan times to be spontaneous, then I already have a non-spontaneous plan in place. And when that plan changes, well, it's frustrating. She listens, smiles and nods, and then tells me I can't plan real spontaneity. What I really need is for my plans to *change*, and this is why I need therapy.

The tension between planners and wingers can cause plenty of stress, but the challenge with faith is that it can't always be planned. Obstacles are always popping up. Changes are always altering the plan, but it's okay when your plans get derailed because God works ahead of you. Your blown plan is God's perfect plan in motion, and the spontaneity is God's planned moment and orchestrated miracle. The Psalmist says of God, "You go before me and follow me. You place your hand of blessing on my head. Such knowledge is too wonderful for me, too great for me to understand!" (Psalm 139:5–6). One of life's great comforts results from believing that God is behind and before you. He protects your blindside. He works in your future to ensure his purpose moves forward through your life for his glory.

God is working ahead in your life, as well. He's already laying the groundwork and making the connections. Faith sometimes means following God even when you don't know where you are going. The most important thing is not knowing all the travel details but traveling with the One who does. The miracle is already in the making.

You may feel a little lost right now, like God isn't showing up. You may feel like you are wandering aimlessly, stuck in the wilderness, but the wilderness is how God prepares you for the promised land. Uncertainty is how God teaches you to live in the certainty of faith. The blessing is already on the way; you just can't see it yet. Step out in faith with his promises as your stepping stones. He is all around you.

UNDERNEATH YOU

Finally, God's presence also means that no matter how far you fall, he is *underneath you*. When you can't go on in your own strength, he carries you along in his. "The eternal God is your refuge, and his everlasting arms are *under* you" (Deuteronomy 33:27). When you hit bottom, you find that God's arms have been there all along. And rock bottom is the foundation on which God rebuilds lives.

I know this firsthand. Every day, I carry my sobriety chip in my pocket. It is gold in color, metal, and a little bigger than a quarter. One side says, "Celebrate Recovery, XXVIII years," and the other says, "My Grace is Sufficient for You." There is nothing special about the chip. I don't carry it because I am chained to my past or because I like to fidget with it. It's kind of a nuisance, always getting in the way when I reach for my keys. Yet, every night before bed I set it by my bathroom sink and every morning I stick it back in my pocket.

Why? Because it reminds me of a time years ago when God's arms caught me—when I called out to him in helplessness as a teenager trapped in a four-year drug addiction. I had no idea if God would even hear, but I prayed for a miracle. Even though I couldn't see it at the time, God was already there. When I hit bottom, his arms were under me. I carry the chip because it reminds me of where God met me, but also of where God has brought me.

The most powerful way to see God's presence is to look back. No matter how far along you are in the faith journey, you can look back to see how God has been with you. In my case, I see God helping me discover his freedom and leading me to a great group of friends who encouraged me at church. He gave me the desire to enter ministry and grew my character and faith. He led me to my wife, the love of my life. He blessed me with two children that I love beyond words. And now I get to share the amazing news of God's grace with others. Every good thing in my life began when I surrendered to God's love.

I keep the chip in my pocket because it represents my experience that God is always with me. It tells me of his faithfulness and humbles me. It states that I'm no better than anyone else, that I've made lots of mistakes, and that I desperately need God and his grace every day. When self-righteousness or a judgmental spirit creeps into my life, it is there, banging around in my pocket. It prompts me to show compassion as I was once shown compassion.

When I get frustrated at other people, and their unwillingness to change, it whispers to me of the times I was unwilling to change. When I want to give up on others, it tells me of others who never gave up on me. When I'm tempted to doubt whether God can do a miracle in someone's life, it shouts of the miracle he did in my life. The chip is a physical reminder of God's presence each day, and it is a reminder I need because, too easily, I forget. I am who I am because he is with me. His grace is sufficient for me. And it is for you, too.

Your Heavenly Father is always with you—over you, by you, in you, around you, and under you. When things feel unhinged, you don't need to be afraid. When you're overwhelmed, you aren't alone. His presence is the promise that fills you with wonder and peace. He's always watching over you to bless and protect. He's gone to crazy lengths to ensure your relationship with him and proven his love in the most dramatic fashion. He's guaranteed that nothing in all the universe can separate you from his presence in Christ.

His presence is his promise.

CHAPTER 2

LITTLE BLUE BOXES AND STAIRWAYS TO HEAVEN

Have you ever gotten something you really wanted and then ended up hating it? Sometimes in these situations we even feel like we get what we deserve, but this kind of thinking is a trap. In order to live in the freedom of God's promises, you have to stop condemning yourself because you have been forgiven.

When I consider this struggle in my own life, I remember the 2005 Ford Mustang I drove for a dozen years. Man, I loved that car! A five-speed stick shift with a white pool cue ball serving as the gear shift handle. Bright red with blacked-out tinted windows, a spoiler on the hood I installed myself, and extra loud mufflers—you could see, and hear, me coming a block away. I justified it as part of my mid-life crisis and congratulated myself that it could have been worse.

But eventually I hated that car. Mainly because of a

small dent in the steering wheel, right in the middle, the size of my knuckle. It resulted from me losing it in traffic one day and punching my steering wheel in a long obnoxious honk—probably at some poor elderly person who had no idea they cut me off.

That dent annoyed me because it represented my flaws, imperfections, and inability to drive like a normal, well-adjusted, calm human being. The dent wasn't the only time I lost my cool, not even close, but it became the visual I stared at every day. I even glued a little logo over the dent, but I still knew it was there, like a challenge: *get a grip on yourself, Pastor Jud.* I finally sold the car for a decidedly nondescript Honda.

That dent was such a small thing, but it shouted to me of an ongoing struggle in my spiritual life. Too often I slip back into old patterns, the residuals of thinking rooted in guilt and self-condemnation. Sometimes I fall back into these patterns after I screw up, like when my impatience gets the best of me in traffic or when I'm too short with my kids; when I don't get my way and pout around like a two-year-old in a grown-up body; after I stick to my health plan for a few days, only to gorge on chicken nachos from *Cheesecake Factory* instead of hitting the gym; or I think something at church should have had a bigger impact than it did. I make the problems all about me and my own insecurity. In general, when I get grumpy, selfish, and hard to live with, something I've done has triggered these guilt-based habits to resurface.

After these moments pass, self-condemnation sets in. I'm disappointed that I didn't handle the situation more maturely. I'm frustrated because I want to honor God with all my heart, but I also want to overeat on nachos. Or I get angry at myself because I don't seem to care at all. I feel guilty that I don't feel *more* guilty! Like I said, old patterns.

And I'm well aware of the problem. Instead of standing on God's Word in these moments, I melt into my feelings. When I'm down or upset, my feelings are like a monster truck pulling me behind with a rope on a skateboard. Trying to brake or slow things down seems like an impossible task. Jumping off looks like it could hurt. I should let go of the rope. I should plant my flag on God's promises, speak God's Word over my life, get away, and pray.

Even after I've done this hundreds of times before and experienced the way it changes the dynamic of the situation, I still struggle. Some days it simply takes too much effort to push back. Sometimes I wonder if I enjoy the self-loathing when I allow my feelings to drag me along, hiding in my shame and playing the martyr.

SHACKLES OF SHAME

Maybe this is all just human experience, and I shouldn't be too hard on myself. After all, the Psalmists sound like their lives are amazing in one Psalm and horrible in the next. Life is up and down for everyone, yet some of this dynamic is rooted in my old life of self-condemnation and guilt. I replay the negative memories of mistakes in my mind. I start to procrastinate key decisions. I don't engage opportunities before me but get paralyzed by obstacles. I parent out of fear rather than faith. I expect more from others than they could possibly give. I stay in condemnation rather than step into God's freedom.

God's presence may be the promise, but sometimes it feels like I deserve to be cut off from his presence because of my own stupidity. I wonder how God could ever put up with a mess like me. I fear that I've disqualified myself from his grace and my selfishness has put me on probation. God may be everywhere to support and forgive his kids, but I've always had a rebellious streak.

Can you relate? Do you find that as much as you hear about forgiveness in Jesus Christ, it's still an idea in your head more than a reality of your heart? Do you believe that God forgives others, but you still wonder, deep down, if he forgives you? Do you get that God loves you, but you still feel like a failure? As a fellow struggler, I can only remind you of what I tell myself: to cling to the amazing promise of God that *there is no condemnation in Christ.*

The remedy for all this self-loathing, guilt, and shame is this monumental assurance: "So now there is no condemnation for those who belong to Christ Jesus" (Romans 8:1). Nothing past or future can cut you off from God's presence through Jesus. Think about that and soak it in. This promise points to what God has done for you in Jesus that allows his presence to dwell with you.

In the last chapter, we considered how God's presence is all around us, specifically to bless and support us no matter what we're going through. This promise of "no condemnation" in Jesus, however, points to what God has done to ensure we can access his presence. This forgiveness is the *what* that allows our relationship with God to be restored.

This restoration promise makes it clear that God knows all about the mind games we play and the ways our enemy can exploit them. The word condemnation here means "to judge someone as definitely guilty and subject to punishment." You have been judged guilty. You've blown it and you know it. You've blown up spectacularly and revealed the ugly, angry, selfishness inside.

Yet, if you trust Jesus with all that you are, there is now no condemnation, absolutely *none*. You are totally, utterly, completely, and categorically outside of the realm of any possible condemnation because you belong to Jesus. Your shackles of shame have been loosed, your cage of contempt has been opened, and you only need to step out into the freedom of our loving God.

His glorious presence is accessible each day through faith—no matter what.

BREAKFAST AT TIFFANY'S

No condemnation isn't a promise out of thin air but one crafted by God himself from the beginning of time. Like an expert jeweler, God has meticulously linked together a stunning chain of circumstances. They create a beautiful masterpiece that ensures his presence dwells freely with you. Your forgiveness and freedom came at great care and cost to God.

It reminds me of being in the mall a while back with some friends when we passed Tiffany & Co., the high-end jeweler.

As the ladies looked in the window, I overheard my wife say, "Every girl dreams of a little blue box from Tiffany's."

Later back at home, I asked her what she meant. She looked at me like I was from *Planet of the Apes*. "You know, that special turquoise shade of blue that's synonymous with Tiffany's—all their jewelry comes in a little box that color. I've dreamed of receiving one since I was a little girl."

This was news to me, but I made a mental note, and when Christmas rolled around, I stopped in to shop for Lori. After looking at the prices, I asked how much it would cost for an *empty* blue box! But I splurged and got her something special and loved seeing the shock on her face when she saw that Tiffany blue box.

Even more precious than anything inside a little blue box from Tiffany's is God's gift of grace. Called the "golden chain" by theologians, it fills us with confidence and bravery to unlock the shackles of our past mistakes and self-condemnation. Paul describes it as the chain of actions that lead to our salvation. He writes: "For those whom [God] *foreknew* he also *predestined* to be conformed to the image of his Son, in order that he might be the firstborn among many brothers. And those whom he predestined he also *called*, and those whom he called he also *justified*, and those whom he justified he also *glorified*" (Roman 8:29-30, ESV, emphasis added). This chain of events is the order of your salvation and freedom: you are foreknown, predestined, called, justified, and glorified. This is all God's doing, and it is glorious.

The first link in the chain is that you are *foreknown*. God knew you from the foundations of the world. You weren't just a twinkle in your parents' eyes when you were born; you were already known by God. A friend recently said that she didn't feel like her friends really knew her. She knew they cared about her, but it felt incomplete, because "to be loved is to be known. If you aren't fully known, you can't be fully loved." She makes an important point.

The term "foreknown" suggests both complete knowledge and love. The Hebrew for "known" implies an intimate knowledge and is equivalent to "love." Those God foreknew are those God fore*loved*.[6] He didn't simply know *of* you, he *loved* you. As Paul writes, "Long before he laid down earth's foundations, he had us in mind, had settled on us as the focus of his love, to be made whole and holy by his love." (Ephesians 1:4, MSG).

You were known and loved from before the beginning. Before your first mistake or sin, before your first disappointment, God already knew. He knows your future sins, as well, and loves you anyway. Your security in salvation begins before the beginning in God, who loved you in spite of your selfishness, temper tantrums, manipulation, and a million other acts you would be embarrassed and ashamed for others to know. And he loved you fully.

The second link of this chain indicates that you are *predestined.* God knew you and loved you, but he also chose you to be in relationship with him. I tease Lori about watching *The Bachelor* with her friends and swooning when he asks one of the contestants, "Will you accept this rose?" Thinking about it, though, I realize the appeal. The rose recipient was *chosen.* She made the cut, and God offers us so much more than just a romantic token. He offers us the power and promise of his eternal love.

Believers have debated whether being chosen means God saw that you would one day believe on your own or whether God chose you to believe and drew you to himself irresistibly. Very smart, educated, and dedicated people fall on both sides of the question. They have disagreed for thousands of years, and the mystery won't be unraveled this side of heaven.

As I've wrestled it through, however, I noticed that Paul doesn't debate the finer points much in his writing in the New Testament. To my reading, he clearly states that God chose you and that's why you are later called and believe. But he also clearly states it is your responsibility to believe. I don't understand all the ins and outs, but Paul seems more concerned with what this means for us practically. As cliché as it may sound, I wonder if it's similar to the old adage about not needing to understand aerodynamics in order to ride in a plane.

Perhaps we don't need to understand, or agree on, all the delineations of what being chosen means as much as we need to focus on the practical outcomes. Nothing fills me with undeserving gratitude like a knowledge that I am chosen by God. I'm driven to my knees in awe, thankfulness, and joy. My spiritual freedom isn't the result of anything in me but everything in God. Why he chose me, or you, I have no idea. But *that* he chose me despite a million reasons why he wouldn't, is something I will never get over. God looked out from all eternity and said, "I chose you. I love you. I pick you."

If that doesn't fill you with wonder, what will?

The third link in the chain is that you are *called*. Remember the story of Lazarus in the Bible? Lazarus was Jesus' friend who passed away. Standing before his tomb, Jesus tells them to roll the stone away. Lazarus's sister, Martha, protests that he has been dead four days, and as the King James Version puts it, "he stinketh" (John 11:39, KJV). (This is a great word when my kids need a shower—you stinketh!) The point is that Lazarus was really, totally, completely *dead*. The Jewish people at that time believed that the soul hovered around the body for three days. When you were four days dead, you were *really* dead. All hope was lost. Nothing could bring you back.

This is a picture of us in our sin. We are four days dead. There is no amount of willpower or inner energy that can help us rise up on our own.

Then Jesus shouts, "Lazarus, come out!" and Lazarus emerges from the grave bound in grave clothes (John 11:43). Jesus first called Lazarus, and *then* he came out. That's how salvation works. He calls and we stand. This distinction is important because a lot of people believe salvation is primarily about personal effort and willpower. Lazarus could not raise himself up. He was dead. We are spiritually dead in our sins, and only when Jesus calls to us can we stand up and come out of whatever tomb sin has left us in.

Then my favorite words in the story: "Jesus told them, 'Unwrap him and let him go!'" (John 11:44). I don't know what you hope for, but this is Jesus' ultimate hope for you.

To call you out of whatever tomb sin has trapped you in. To say let her go, unwrap her, and set her free! Unwrap him and turn him loose to live. Jesus is still unwrapping people. He can unwrap you from what binds you, from the pain of your broken identity, from your sin to release you into resurrection. And just like Lazarus, he calls you to life.

The fourth link in the chain means you are *justified*. You have moved from accused to affirmed. Anyone who has ever been sued, ticketed, or gotten into some kind of dispute knows how painful it is to be accused; to have your character and actions called into question. All you want is for someone to come along and affirm you, to say you are in the right. Justified is literally a legal term, and that's what Jesus did for you and me on a cosmic scale even though we were in the wrong.

We are all guilty and constantly accused by the evil one. In fact, one of his names is simply the Accuser, but the trial is over and Jesus declares you innocent. You are fully vindicated, not based on the evidence against you, but on the evidence of Christ's righteousness. He received the not-guilty verdict, and by grace through faith, his rightful verdict falls to you. John Stott writes, "The essence of sin is man substituting himself for God, while the essence of salvation is God substituting himself for man."[7] Jesus substitutes himself and his goodness for you. Grace reigns in your life because you have been justified.

The last link completing the majestic chain reveals you are *glorified*. This link points to the final hope you have of being fully conformed to Christ's image. The term glorified looks to heaven. The word is past tense, like each link on the chain, and suggests it has already happened, even though our experience of it is still future. God's process of salvation is so sure it is described as already being complete. You are being changed, but one day you will ultimately be changed. God will see it through to the end. Paul says, "And I am certain that God, who began the good work within you, will continue his work until it is finally finished on the day when Christ Jesus returns" (Philippians 1:6). God completes what he starts. When he begins to work in your life, he never abandons his labor. He never becomes lazy or neglectful and sees it through until the end.

When the Bible says there is "no condemnation," all of this meaning is behind it. When we throw around the word "grace," these links are what hold it together. A beautiful golden chain moving from one link to the next by God: *fore-*loved, *predestined, called, justified,* and *glorified.* God did it all! He secured your freedom in every possible way. You are no longer accused; you have been declared righteous. And no matter how you feel, you're part of the most important, most blessed, most amazing event in history—the salvation of all who believe.

STAIRWAY TO HEAVEN

You are absolutely set free from condemnation by the will of God from the foundation of the world. The power of the past, and the penalty of your sin, has been utterly demolished by the golden chain of salvation. Your freedom has been secured—*forever*. The challenge, however, is to live in freedom rather than to revert to old patterns of condemnation and self-defeat conditioned by your past. These old habits keep us feeling caged even though God has blown the doors wide open.

Too often, we're like our family bulldog Roxy—a pudgy, brown and white, lovable thing with a smushed-up face. Rather than drink from her clean, fresh dish of water that we provide daily, she sneaks away to another source—the toilet! Seriously, what's up with *that*?

Yet we often do the same thing when we don't use our freedom wisely. We seek our security from the promises of the world. We turn to pleasure, power, or accomplishment to fill needs that only God can fill. We depend on ourselves and our good deeds to ensure our right standing with God. We go back to our old patterns of self-condemnation when we have been categorically freed in Jesus. It is like bypassing the fresh, amazing river of God's mercy, for what, in comparison, is a bowl of serious yuck, and the aftertaste has nasty effects for our lives.

Living in condemnation often shows itself in unexpected ways like self-sabotage. You say things you don't mean to push people away you wish would stay close. This response ensures the loneliness that you desperately don't want to experience.

You quit or transfer before a long-awaited promotion. In the back of your mind, you hear a family member who always said you were nothing. You don't believe them, but your actions suggest otherwise.

You hate the pressure you are under, so you take steps that ensure your own downfall. You don't admit this is happening, but you suspend consequences for your actions and withdraw from friends and colleagues who could help.

You refuse to get counseling for problems blowing up your life. You tell yourself you can handle it when you know you simply can't. You don't want to open the door to the junk of the past, but that door is already wide open. The past is tumbling out and undermining everything you hope about the future. All of these patterns signal that you aren't fully embracing your freedom.

If you don't deal *with* the pain of the past, you deal *out* that pain in your present. If you don't deal with the pain of abandonment, you may deal out that pain and leave when others need you most. If you don't deal with the pain of abuse, you may deal out that abuse to those you swore to never hurt. If you don't deal with the rejection, you may deal out harsh words to those who look to you for affirmation and acceptance. God's freedom is there for the taking, but you have to access it freely.

You were meant for the incredible chain of God's freedom to grace your neck, but instead the past and its condemnation have become a heavy chain of captivity. So after Paul lays out the golden chain of salvation, he asks five questions to reinforce the spiritual freedom you have in Jesus. These questions move your understanding from head to heart. They form a stairway to heaven, leading to the highest places of trust and grace.

The first question is, "*If God is for us, who can be against us?"* (Romans 8:31, ESV). Throughout my entire ministry at Central Church, I've closed out every service with this question. Even today across our locations, this is the last statement people hear each weekend as they leave. This isn't a question seeking an answer but a statement demanding a response.

Yes, God is for you as followers of Jesus. God is for your maturity, freedom, holiness, blessing, joy, character, and purpose. God is for you in your normalcy and oddity and in your oddities that you consider normal. He is for you in your outgoing, boisterous, tame, or conservative personality. He is for you with or without tattoos, piercings, long hair, or short. He is for you in your suburban house, urban apartment, or prison cell. He is for you in your trendy outfit or hopelessly un-trendy one that will eventually come back around. And since this incredible reality is true, who can stand against you?

On the surface a lot of things may stand against you—people, situations, crises, and circumstances. Paul describes these realities around this verse in terms like "groaning," "persecution," and "hardship." But he's looking beyond this and asking ultimately, who can prevail against you? If God is God, then nothing can stop his plan, prevent his love, or hold back his work in your life. The God of the universe is for you; the one who spins the earth on its axis and holds the stars in place; the one who formed you in the womb and tweaked your DNA; the one whose promise is true; who loved you ahead of time, chose you, called you, justified you, and will glorify you. He moves and works on your behalf. *God* is *for* you!

When you believe God is for you and really believe it, everything changes. Every problem takes on a different light. The hardship becomes something that perfects your faith and draws you close to God. The test transforms into an opportunity to prepare for God's future blessing. The difficulty is a tool in God's hands to make you stronger and wiser. The lessons from the pain empower you to fulfill your purpose.

My response to this amazing statement is thanks and praise. I am unworthy. On my own I fail miserably, but I will never be on my own again. I'm a mess, but I am absolutely God's mess. I am often difficult to love, but God loves me in spite of me, and he loves you in spite of you. Nothing ultimately can stand against you!

PRICELESS BEYOND COMPARE

Paul's second question is, *"He who did not spare his own Son but gave him up for us all, how will he not also with him graciously give us all things?"* (Romans 8:32, ESV). This question gets to a deeper logic that backs up the first question. God gave his one and only Son for you. How can he not also give you what you need? The argument is from great to less. If God did the greater thing, giving up his Son, how would he not also do the lesser thing, meet your need?

God demonstrated his love in the most surprising and unexpected way on the cross. Early Christians found the cross so disturbing that they did not use it as a main symbol of the faith. It wasn't until the fifth century, or over 100 years after crucifixion was made illegal, that crosses began to appear as markers for faith in carvings and paintings.[8] The act of crucifixion was so ruthless, and conjured up such graphic brutality, that it took a century after it was banned for believers to represent their faith with a cross.

Imagine Jesus, already beaten and bloodied, hanging on that horrible cross, that instrument of torture, that ancient form of the hangman's noose, guillotine, or electric chair—except so much more gruesome. God allowed his own Son to endure this for your sake. If Jesus went through that kind of horrific pain, if God would go that far, there is *nothing* he wouldn't do. In fact, there is nothing he hasn't already done!

Jesus was willing to endure so much pain, heartache, and suffering for you. When you consider this, is it not crazy that you and I worry so much about things like rent, or car payments, or whether we've saved enough for the kids' college? Are we not questioning God's love in all this worry and fear? Does it not seem ludicrous when you consider all he did on the cross? If he did all this for you, he *will* meet your need. Stand on it, believe it, claim it, receive it!

THE FINAL SAY

Paul's third question is, "*Who shall bring any charge against God's elect?* It is God who justifies" (8:33, ESV). Lots of people may accuse you. Sometimes the voice in your head tells you, *God will never forgive you. God doesn't care. The Church doesn't love you.* Others may accuse you of not being enough as a friend, family member, or employee. The devil wants nothing more than to keep you weighed down by a rap sheet from your past or to keep you indifferent and numb to God because of your own condemnation.

But ultimately it is God's opinion that matters. He is the one who justifies or declares you just and right. Through faith in Jesus you are made right with God based on Jesus' righteousness and not your own. Don't let your failures cloud Jesus' work in your heart. You are God's chosen and no accusation stands against you.

"*Who is to condemn?*" Paul's fourth question carries over from the last. He answers, "Christ Jesus is the one who died—more than that, who was raised—who is at the right hand of God, who indeed is interceding for us" (8:34, ESV). Only Jesus can ultimately condemn, and in him, there is no condemnation. He intercedes for you as your mediator and stands in the gap. You are free to laugh and love. Free to be imperfect but awesome, flawed but faithful, messy but a masterpiece. You are free to be you, the one and only you. Other people don't get to shackle you to their ideal of who you should be. Others don't get to control the script unless you empower them. You are God's, and you are free.

Finally, Paul asks, "*Who shall separate us from the love of Christ?*" (8:35, ESV). These questions build, like we are climbing to the top, the stairway to heaven. The answer is implied. No one and nothing—absolutely nothing. Not your pain, mistakes, addiction, divorce, or broken family; not your kid who continues to rebel; not your secret sin, darkest memory, troubled present, or difficult future. None of it separates you from the love of Christ.

In Christ, you're not your worst moments. You're not what happened to you. You're not a victim, mistake, or accident. Think of when you rebelled, shaded the truth, and went your own way. God still pursued you, wooed you, and drew you back to himself. Think of when you needed his love and forgiveness most, and deserved it least, and he was still faithful. Remember how he rescued you when you had nothing to offer him and nothing to give. Recall his love that is so bold, beautiful, powerful, awesome, amazing, and majestic; there aren't enough words! Let God forgive the past, carry the burden, and heal the bitterness. Learn from the past, but don't be imprisoned by it. Release the past so you don't repeat it. Drink deeply from the fresh water of God's freedom.

TRUST ISSUES

How I access the freedom that God has accomplished for me centers on my trust. And trust can be a challenging thing when I have something at stake, like I learned at the dentist.

I grew up drinking well water in Texas as a kid, and it discolored my front teeth. So I've had plenty of dental work done to the point where I'm traumatized by visits to the dentist's office. When I got out of college, I had veneers put over my front teeth. They actually shaved part of my existing teeth down and then glued veneers over what was left of my teeth.

Once I bit into some bread at dinner with friends. To my absolute horror, my entire veneer came off my right front tooth. I stared at it in shock sticking out of that piece of bread. Before anyone could notice, I put the veneer in my pocket. I looked like a half vampire with one shaved front fang and one normal tooth.

For the rest of the night I laughed at jokes and smiled without opening my mouth. The next day I made an emergency appointment with the dentist who glued it back on. Even though it was repaired, I no longer trusted it to stay. I ate things very gently and avoided too much pressure on that tooth when biting. I kept having this recurring nightmare that I was speaking somewhere, and in the middle of my talk my front tooth flew off into the audience. Everybody gasped. People ran out of the building. There was my face on a giant Jumbotron, toothless for the world to see.

As an out-of-town speaking engagement drew near, my worry increased about the state of my tooth. I couldn't let it go, so I went to see the dentist again.

He asked, "Is it giving you any problems? Does it feel loose?"

"No, but I'm still afraid it will pop off," I answered. He looked at me strangely and grabbed a tool that looked like pliers you get at the hardware store. He pulled and pushed on my front tooth with force and said, "It is rock solid, Jud—it isn't coming off."

"I know this isn't rational. I am sure you are right, but I just don't trust it. I need some big-time, amazing, incredible glue to make sure the thing doesn't pop off. I can't be toothless on a big screen. Can you help me here?"

He finally gave in and glued the veneer again.

When he was finished, I asked, "Can you send me home with some bonding glue just in case it does pop off, so I can glue it back on myself until I get back to town?"

My dentist looked at me and smiled. He said, "I could do that, but I will not." Then he paused and added, "You have to *trust me*." I laughed nervously.

Back in my car driving home, it occurred to me that this is like the life of faith. God is saying, "You have to trust me. You have to choose to let go of all the fear, worry, and self-condemnation and believe in what I accomplished for you in your heart. I won't take that worry away, but you can release it with trust, and you can experience freedom." It is a daily faith decision, one I exercise not only in my relationship with God, but also in my dentist, which is why I'm smiling without worry as I write.

Do you dare trust the depth of this promise?

There is no condemnation for the time you lied to cover your tracks or exaggerated to look more impressive. No condemnation for when you let jealousy get the better of you or when you weren't there for a friend or loved one; when you lost your cool and let your words fly; when you were unfaithful in a relationship; when the marriage fell apart; when you weren't there as a parent; when you hid the credit card from your spouse; when the prescription pills became a habit; when sexual sins consumed you. There is no condemnation for lust, for the gossip passed on at another's expense, for fudging the numbers and believing the end justified the means. No condemnation for when you drank too much, for the lies you told yourself and others about an addiction, for that time you told God you would never do it again, and then you did it again; for the time you promised God you would do something, but then you didn't.

Are you walking in this liberation? Or are you carrying around that old guilt and shame you've asked God to forgive a hundred times? Are you still walking around afraid that you aren't enough? Are you still chained to the past by chains that God has already unlocked?

In Christ, the old has gone and the new has come. You are a new creation. It's a new day filled with new promise, hope, possibilities and opportunities, new dreams, goals, perspective, and resolve. God's mercy is new every morning. His grace is fresh every day. His love is poured out. His Spirit is working. Great is his faithfulness! He does not treat you as your sins deserve!

As Paul wrote in what must be some of the most powerful words ever written for a believer, it just doesn't get any better than this:

> And I am convinced that nothing can ever separate us from God's love. Neither death nor life, neither angels nor demons, neither our fears for today nor our worries about tomorrow—not even the powers of hell can separate us from God's love. No power in the sky above or in the earth below—indeed, nothing in all creation will

> ever be able to separate us from the love of God that is revealed in Christ Jesus our Lord (Romans 8:38–39).

Read them again, pray over them, and reflect on them until your heart is moved. Wear the golden chain of salvation on your heart. Stand in the promise that guarantees God's presence.

There. Is. No. Condemnation.

CHAPTER 3

A BREATH OF FRESH AIR

So far we have seen that God's big promise is his presence. His presence is with us—over, by, in, around, and underneath us. He fills us with wonder, gives us boldness and courage, and allows us to walk freely as his people. Thanks to the "golden chain" of salvation, the freedom movement that God put into place since before the beginning, there is no condemnation. You have free access to God's presence.

All of this is *what* God has done for you through Jesus. The way you receive this, the *how,* is through the power of the Holy Spirit. God strengthens your life as you rely more and more on his Spirit dwelling in you—especially at times when you simply can't go on. You can take great comfort from God's promise: *I will send my Spirit.*

Like the time when Lori convinced me to join her for a workout guided by one of her exercise videos. I resisted because her program seemed specifically made for women.

This wasn't Tony Horton's famously intense P90X, and there were no ex-green berets or cage fighters barking instructions. No, instead participants used small foamy weights that didn't go above ten pounds while listening to a pleasant woman who reminded me of an elementary school teacher.

"This is going to be too easy," I thought to myself, "but I'll say yes to make Lori happy." So I shut the blinds to be sure no one could see me and grabbed my neon-blue hand weight. I stood next to my wife in front of a TV screen and she hit play.

After five minutes, I was in *serious* trouble.

That little hand weight suddenly felt like fifty pounds. My lungs were burning and I couldn't catch my breath. Everything hurt. The ladies in the video received the full force of my frustration, and I called them out on their lies, "You said, 'just a couple more,' five minutes ago!" By the time the session was over, I was on my back, sucking wind. I literally could not move, much less think of ever walking again! Lori, however, barely broke a sweat.

I'd envisioned myself to be a pretty strong person, but when I was put to the test, I just didn't have it in me. (This experience did motivate me, however, to work my way up to P90X—it took a very long time!) Sooner or later, life leaves all of us feeling the same way, drained and powerless.

You gave it all you had and it wasn't enough. You threw everything at the problem and it wouldn't get better. You tried your best and still no breakthrough. You prayed and prayed and the darkness didn't lift. You're trying to get through life, but there's not much life flowing through you.

Eventually, I did get up off the floor after that deceptively intense workout. My heart stopped racing. My mind cleared up. Strength returned to my aching limbs, but only after a lot of breathing in and out. Getting back on my feet took time.

If you are tired, worn out, flat on your back, maybe it's time to breathe again, spiritually. Just as your physical life needs oxygen to survive, your spiritual life needs the Holy Spirit to stay energized. And the good news is that you have access to God's Holy Spirit—he's promised!

SCRAPING THE WALL

A lack of understanding and relying on God's Spirit is one of the regrets of my early faith journey. For too long, I treated God's Spirit like an afterthought. I relied on my own strength rather than the Holy Spirit's. I confessed my faith in God but confronted my problems in my own power. I believed God could do great things, but I didn't activate my faith and depend on him to do those great things. I failed to fully experience and live in the promised Spirit and the promised presence.

You cannot live the life God has for you on your own steam. Your new life is powered by the grace, love, and ability that flow through the divine person of the Holy Spirit. You've got to remember to breathe, spiritually, and be filled by his Spirit. Otherwise, you'll end up depleted and exhausted, defeated by your default tendency to go it alone.

I know this too well. As I mentioned in the Introduction,

a few years ago I was on a collision course with burnout. What I experienced was more than simple fatigue or needing a vacation. If you're worn out, time off can recharge you, but not so with burnout. It's an exhaustion compounded by emptiness and spiraling into darkness. It's being emotionally overdrawn and spiritually undersupplied. When you hit full-on burnout, there's a good chance you won't bounce back from it with the energy and vigor you had before, especially in the area that caused it.

Red flags popped up in my life. The most jarring occurred after a baptism celebration service with new believers. Nothing fires me up like seeing people trust Jesus for their salvation or follow through with baptism. After watching hundreds of people be baptized, I felt . . . *nothing*. I was intellectually excited for them but emotionally numb. I drove home and realized how serious things were in my heart.

So I began to examine my life. I'd allowed my prayer life to slide for an extended period. I've never been great at sticking to set times of prayer and am at my best when I'm praying throughout the day. I couldn't remember the last time I had asked God to fill me with his Spirit. I had been going for too long from task to task without personally depending on God. The resulting strain began to wear me down. Bitterness took root in my heart and began to grow.

My heart was drifting and becoming cynical. I took on too much travel, too many projects, and didn't manage my schedule with common sense. My old familiar impatience was rearing its head again. Most of us will circle around the same personality and sin patterns throughout our lives.

God's Spirit can bring victory, but this doesn't mean these patterns won't rear their heads again in different seasons, especially when we are vulnerable.

For me, a lack of appropriate boundaries with my schedule and a fierce ability to focus and work are both a strength and a weakness. I have struggled with these my entire adult life with varying degrees of success. My "addictive personality" that once led me down a destructive path of substance abuse shifted its focus to work. Yet something about my depth of emotional numbness startled me. I feared I might break apart like Humpty Dumpty and never get put back together again the same way.

I'd watched friends burnout, so I knew I needed to take action. So I talked to my wife, spiritual advisors, and friends, being honest about things that needed to change, and I sought accountability with my schedule. I worked with Lori to create a "stop doing list." I quit traveling for an extended season. While I've always enjoyed writing, I took an indefinite sabbatical. I gave myself to core tasks of being a husband, father, and local pastor. I got more intentional about my relationship with God.

I also worked with a spiritual advisor for an extended period. He's a Christian psychologist and doesn't like to be called a counselor, but that's what he is to me. After several months he told me, "Jud, you didn't hit the burnout wall head on, but you did sideswipe it pretty good, like an Indy driver who makes the turn but scrapes the wall."

I learned that when you're that depleted, the last thing you have is perspective, especially on how depleted you are. You run out of perspective long before you run out of road and crash. He helped me see that my most important job was not to serve, teach, or lead but simply to breathe. I needed to let God love me again. I needed his Spirit to fill me anew.

I did bounce back, but it was eighteen months before I began to feel like myself again—long enough to fear that I might never recover. But I'll never forget the joy I felt one Saturday while preparing for our weekend church services. There was nowhere I'd rather be. Nothing I'd rather be doing. No one I'd rather be with than the people of our church. I felt energized, alive, strong, and at peace.

Throughout this entire process, the most important part was God's Spirit. He breathed new life into my weary heart. I experienced the way God's Spirit brings life, not just for salvation, but for every day if we depend on him and seek his guidance and gifting.

NEW LIFE FOR DRY BONES

My experience reminds me of one passage in the Old Testament that serves as both a prophetic vision and a metaphor for God's Spirit's work. In it, we see new life brought by God. The prophet Ezekiel is carried away in a vision and sees a valley filled with nothing but dry bones. It must have resembled something like *Night of the Living Dead*—only it seemed real.

God asks Ezekiel, "Can these bones live?" (Ezekiel 37:3, ESV). In any other circumstances, and with anyone else asking the question, the answer would be, "No." The bones are hard, dried out, and lifeless. Used up and forgotten, these dry bones can never live again.

We've probably all had moments that felt this way—when things just can't be restored. A marriage withers and love slowly dies. A dream burns itself into nothing but cold ashes. A career ends after an irretrievable mistake. A person of faith drifts farther and farther from God, neglecting the lifelines all around her. A divisive and quarrelling church can feel like a valley of bones, as well: void of love and the life-giving grace of God.

But Ezekiel knows not to underestimate God. Nothing is impossible for God. He answers, "O Lord God, you know" (37:3, ESV). Only God can raise the dead. Only God can give new life where life has gone. Only God can bring something beautiful from what looks wasted.

Then Ezekiel is told to prophesy to the bones: "Dry bones, listen to the word of the LORD! This is what the Sovereign LORD says: 'Look! I am going to put breath into you and make you live again!'" (37:4-5). Here we see the power of God's breath to give life and purpose to what is lost. Suddenly, a deafening, rattling noise exploded across the valley. Skeletons came together, muscles and tendons attached, and skin formed over the bodies. And you thought *The Walking Dead* was scary! In the vision, corpses formed, but they were not yet living for God had not breathed into them.

Ezekiel says, "This is what the Sovereign LORD says: 'Come, O breath, from the four winds! Breathe into these dead bodies so they may live again'" (37:9). Here we see breath and wind as the pictures of God's Spirit equipped with the power to give life. Immediately, breath came into their bodies and they stood up as a great army of people.

The prophetic message to Ezekiel is that the people of Israel had become like dry bones. These were people of faith who believed in God, but their nation was destroyed. They were exiled and all hope was gone, but God was not finished. He would fill those bones again with his presence. He would restore their nation, give them hope, and renew their purpose. Some commentators see in this vision the still future restoration of Israel at Christ's return, yet the beginning fulfillment of what God has set in motion is seen throughout the New Testament. God reveals to Ezekiel that this will involve a new covenant and an everlasting ruler, both of which point to Christ and the work he began.

While this story is prophecy, it's also a metaphor of what God's Spirit does in our lives. Before faith, you were not simply a little sick, you were dead. Paul says, "Once you were dead because of your disobedience and your many sins. . . But God is so rich in mercy, and he loved us so much, that even though we were dead because of our sins, he gave us life when he raised Christ from the dead. (It is only by God's grace that you have been saved!)" (Ephesians 2:1, 4–5).

Your sins didn't leave you with the flu; they left you dead as dry bones baked in the desert sun. There are no natural solutions to the problem of death. Only God and his Spirit can animate what is dead. Through faith in Christ and his work, God raises you to new life. Your dry bones can live again, both in salvation and in renewal.

This story is a picture of what God did in my life in salvation and what he did again in my renewal. Your heart can live again, as well. Your life can move forward in God's power. You are not left to scrape along in your own strength. God is available if you will only cry out to him, ask him to fill you, and depend on him.

If you want to live in freedom, then invite his Spirit to breathe new life into your dry bones.

BETTER THAN JESUS

The importance of God's Spirit can't be overstated. In fact, Jesus told his followers it was best that he went away, so that the Holy Spirit would come (see John 16:7). We may romanticize the time of Christ and wish we were there in person to see him, yet Jesus implies that it is better for us to live in this age, after his crucifixion, resurrection, and ascension to heaven. In this time, his Spirit is available in a powerful way to guide us and help us. He told his followers, "But when the Father sends the Advocate as my representative—that is, the Holy Spirit—he will teach you everything and will remind you of everything I have told you" (John 14:26).

The term "advocate" as a designation for the Holy Spirit is difficult to capture in a single English word. So the term is translated "helper," "comforter," and "counselor" in various Bible translations. The word literally means "to come alongside" and referred to an attorney who was kept on retainer by a family. If legal troubles arose, the attorney would be called on to come and provide help, counsel, and insight.[9]

The Holy Spirit works the same way in our lives today. He guides, counsels, comforts, and helps us in the challenges of everyday life. He brings God's Word to life in our hearts and minds and empowers us to exercise our gifts for God's glory.

God's Spirit gives you gifts and empowers you to use those gifts in service to him. He convicts you of your sin and fills you with joy in your salvation. He gives assurance of your salvation and right standing with God and pours in courage when you face opposition, but the greatest thing he gives is simply *life*. The Spirit always brings life.

What could happen if you daily asked God to fill you with his Spirit? What kind of turnarounds could you experience if you stopped trying to turn things around in your own power? What could be different if you asked God to make these dry bones alive again with his presence and power?

POWER UNDER CONTROL

The word often used in the original Hebrew for Spirit literally means "breath" or "wind." And while you may not think of breath as very powerful, the wind is another story. In the Mojave Desert, where I live, we get 300-plus days of sunshine. We don't get much rain, snow, or any other kind of weather events, but we do get wind. Powerful, unbridled wind.

One of the strongest windstorms in recent memory had gusts of over sixty miles per hour. So much dust blew up that visibility was reduced to nothing. Power lines were knocked out; trees and signs blew over. An eighteen-wheeler was toppled over on the freeway. I heard of one resident whose full-sized trampoline was wrenched free from its anchor bolts, hurled across the street, and implanted itself into a neighbor's exterior wall.

Everything shakes under this kind of wind, from windows to fixtures to what's left of the backyard patio furniture. When the wind blows like this for hours, it feels apocalyptic, like the end of the world and can literally put "the fear of God" in you. So to me it's quite significant that "wind" is the word used to describe the Holy Spirit.

The first time the Spirit is signified in the Bible comes in the second verse of Genesis. We read, "The earth was formless and empty, and darkness covered the deep waters. And the Spirit of God was hovering over the surface of the waters" (Genesis 1:2). Not surprisingly, the word rendered "Spirit" here is often translated as *wind*. Scholars debate whether this line should actually read "the wind of God" was over the waters.[10]

Wind is an incredibly powerful and uninhibited force and represents the sheer strength and power of God. From the opening lines of the Bible, it's clear that the Spirit is not domesticated or tame. Our Creator does not fit inside the small boxes we set up for him. Like a hurricane, invisible but incredibly powerful, the Spirit has a mighty strength with which no one can reckon.

Like the wind, Jesus says the Spirit blows where he wants (see John 3:8). And at Pentecost when the church began in Acts, the Spirit arrives in what sounds like a mighty windstorm (see Acts 2:2). The name "Holy Spirit" only magnifies this sense of power. Holy means "to cut" or "separate," literally "a cut above." God is a cut above and beyond us; he is categorically "other." The term holy can't be reduced to moral superiority because God's holiness implies that he is transcendent in every way, including all his attributes and characteristics. To call him the Holy Spirit means his power, influence, and purity are utterly other. We don't have the capacity to fully revere all he is.

Yet this mighty wind also "hovers" over the water. The Hebrew idea behind hovering "suggests the action of a bird covering or nestling over its brood"—a tender image of power under control, sustaining care, and even intimacy—which brings out the other meaning of the Hebrew word for Spirit: breath.[11]

Breath is what we need to survive. We cannot go for more than a few minutes without breathing or we will die. Heck, just blowing up my kids' balloons for a birthday party leaves me hyperventilating! Breath is essential to our life. God *breathed* life into Adam in the Garden, and Jesus *breathed* the Spirit onto the disciples after his resurrection. Breath gets to what is closest within us. It's literally what is most immanent to us. God's Spirit is as close as our own breath. In him we live and move and have our being. We depend on breath every moment of every day.

God's Spirit is both untamed and principled, powerful and gentle, expansive and immanent, literally "wind" and "breath." These two symbols suggest dimensions of our atmosphere, from whirling windstorms to peaceful breezes to the air we breathe. God's Spirit is present in all of this. He's as available as oxygen, as evident as clouds racing across the sky. The Spirit is present, he works and moves in and around us, but he is also separate. He brings resources from beyond.

As God's Spirit becomes known through the Bible, more symbols are used for him like fire, water, oil, cloud, light, and a dove. At Jesus' baptism, the Spirit descended like a dove, which alludes back to the "hovering" in Genesis 1:2. In that creation moment, we see the Spirit do what he does over and over again. He brings order from chaos, form and function from dysfunction. He brings the old creation into being but also the new creation into our own hearts. He makes all things new.

The picture of the Spirit hovering over the waters when the earth was "formless and empty, and darkness covered the deep waters" remains a powerful image for what the Spirit still does. The heart can be a place of darkness and chaos, one which can feel formless, empty, and sick—a place in deep need of care and renewal.

Sometimes you don't know what ails you; you just know something isn't right. You feel unwell. You don't need a vacation. You don't need an attitude adjustment. You don't need to go into more debt, or find a new romance, or find a new anything. You need the Spirit to brood upon your darkness. He brings new creation to your chaos. He crafts beauty from ashes. He calls new life from what appears dead with both mighty power and tender intimacy. Breath and wind. Power under control.

Paul said of the Spirit that he knows all things and makes known to us the deeper things of God (see 1 Corinthians 2:11). He is available to help you in your weaknesses and sustain you with every breath. He is filled with love toward you and can ensure you are never alone and never without resources to face whatever you are up against.

STAY UN-THIRSTY, MY FRIENDS

God's Spirit is not only wind and breath but also water. The human body can only survive without water for three days. Drinking is something you do a lot. Dos Equis' The Most Interesting Man in the World says, "Stay thirsty, my friends." This request is not a problem because you are constantly feeling and quenching your thirst.

That's why it's so significant that water is a symbol of the Holy Spirit. He's not only breath, something you need constantly and don't think about much. He is also water, something you crave and drink in regularly. Jesus makes this point in a dramatic fashion.

A popular public festival was underway in Jerusalem called the Feast of Tabernacles. Jews from all over the world came in for this weeklong celebration that acted out many aspects of the Exodus from Egypt. For instance, they built temporary shelters and had a kind of camp out to symbolize their ancestors' wilderness wanderings. It culminated in a grand finale where priests brought some water from the Pool of Siloam and poured it out on the altar. This represented the water God miraculously provided for his people during their time in the desert. It celebrated God's provision in their time of need. It was a big deal.

And it was around this moment, most likely, that Jesus

stood up and shouted these words to the large crowds: "Anyone who is thirsty may come to me! Anyone who believes in me may come and drink! For the Scriptures declare, 'Rivers of living water will flow from his heart'" (John 7:38). Jesus offered himself to the thirsty.

John lets us know that Jesus was not simply talking about water. He was talking about the Spirit, and he was issuing a challenge that remains today. We can either lean into religion and ritual that celebrates what God has done in the past, or we can drink in what God is doing today. A crowd of people watched some water get poured out until it ran dry. Jesus offered the Spirit to be poured into them without ever running out. He offered a joy that would well up and spill out as goodness. No wonder he shouted! He wanted people to taste and see that the Lord was good.

Jesus had mentioned this water earlier saying, "Those who drink the water I give will never be thirsty again. It becomes a fresh, bubbling spring within them, giving them eternal life" (John 4:14). The term Jesus uses for the flowing of water indicates that it isn't simply a stream that bubbles forth in the rainy season. He is describing a continual stream of water that leads to eternal life. It's more than just life that doesn't stop, literally "unending real life."[12] And it's not just life as you know it now, but a deeper, more satisfying, and dynamic life.

LIFE AT THE NEXT LEVEL

What do you *really* want?

It's a powerful question, and one that motivates nearly every choice and action, often without you thinking about it much. But in order to understand the abundant life that Jesus came to bring, consider for a moment, right here and now, what you really want.

Some immediate solutions or fixes may come to mind: money, so you wouldn't have to work so hard or to pay off bills and get out of debt; reconciliation in a strained relationship; or healing for an ongoing health issue. Or it might be something really simple, even mundane—for the dog to stop barking next door; for your kids to clean their rooms; for your spouse to notice you and really see what's going on inside you. Maybe you just want a good night's sleep. There is always something you long for, some fulfillment to a pressing need.

But what is *beyond* the pressing need? When the bills, the challenging people, health, kids, and everything else gets resolved, then what? What do you want then? What's the über desire of your life, the *long* want? Whatever it is, I'm pretty certain it represents something about what it means to experience life to the fullest.

Life is a funny word, and in fact, the Greek language in biblical times had three different words that all get translated as *life* in English.[13] The first was the word *bios*, which means life in the most generic sense. Every living thing from an amoeba to a human has *bios*. This is where we get our word biology. This meaning is not the word Jesus used. He didn't say, "I am the water that gives life to merely keep your body functioning."

The second word for life in the Greek language was *psyche*, which usually referred to intelligent life. It's where we get our word psychology. It means "the normal range of human activity." It's like when you ask people how they like their job, and they say, "It's a living." It means they're getting by, surviving, but Jesus didn't say, "I am water of surviving."

This last word for life is the one that Jesus chose—*zoe*. It has an aspect of higher quality to it. It's a whole other level of living. You aren't just existing; you aren't just surviving, but you are truly *living*. You are alive to God and all the things he has for you. This life is the kind of life Jesus offers. It's the life the Spirit produces. It's the kind of life we crave because it's the very life we're made for.

Studies show that if your basic needs are met, you immediately move on to other needs in your life that become very prevalent. You long for security, influence, purpose, and love. These are spiritual needs. You often look to fill these needs with physical things. You have these desires and cravings that well up in your heart. How do you deal with them? You go shopping, play golf, or go for a night out.

But don't try to satisfy spiritual thirst with non-spiritual things. All you will do is patch it up for a little while. It will never be enough. C.S. Lewis once said, "Nearly all that we call human history—money, poverty, ambition, war, prostitution, classes, empires, slavery—is the long, terrible story of man trying to find something other than God which will make him happy."[14]

In essence, Jesus is challenging us, "If you want to be satisfied with life at the next level, that fulfillment comes from me through the Spirit. I am the water of life. I am the bread of life. Come to me for security, relationship, provision, adventure, purpose, and power." You desperately need the love of God in Jesus Christ bubbling up inside of you by the Spirit and overflowing out of your life into other people's lives.

Here is how I've seen Christ's life bubble up in my own life. First, I received forgiveness of my sins. I was set free from the past. In many ways, this is a continual process. God declares me righteous by faith, but I still need to work out my past, my mistakes, and my failures. I process them. I grow past them. I get stronger. I actually *want* to be better. That's the new life coming through. God's Spirit slowly grows a new character in me.

Another way I see Christ's life coming through is by serving. The Holy Spirit fills each follower of Jesus with gifts so that they can give practical help and guidance to the Church, which is Christ's body. Life flows through you as you engage your gifts and give back. This giving back can happen informally as you interact with family and friends, but I believe the main purpose of a gift is to connect us to a local church. The church is where your new life in Christ finds clear expression.

A third way to embrace this *zoe*, life, is simply being able to sense the joy, peace, and love of God's presence. I used to be an angry person. I had little patience or compassion for others. I battled addiction with all the self-centered destruction that comes along with that lifestyle. Left to my own plan, I'd have either wound up in prison or six feet under, but God's Spirit got a hold of me, and now I'm more patient. I love to see life change. I still struggle with things like everyone, but it dawned on me one day that I don't have any enemies. It's incredibly freeing. People may consider me their enemy, but I can't control how people think about me. I can only respond with how I think about them. I don't have any enemies and that freedom feels like life. That's the life Jesus came to bring you and me. It's a little bit of heaven right now here on earth.

SURRENDER TO BE FILLED

So how do we get this new, next-level life? The Bible offers a clear instruction: *be filled*. And here is where we hit upon one of the mysteries of our faith. The Spirit is alive and active. He is everywhere, and when you accept Christ and place your faith in him, he sends you his Spirit. So there is one sense in which you always have the Spirit, but Paul commands believers to be filled, or "to always be being filled" with the Spirit (see Ephesians 5:18).

For me, to be filled with the Spirit begins the moment I wake up. Not every day, but on my best days, before my feet hit the floor, I ask the Holy Spirit to fill me. Then throughout the day I try to be sensitive to what the Spirit is saying and where he is leading. I can overpower this inner voice very easily. I can get distracted. I can pull the ripcord on certain conversations I feel led to have. I can be like Jonah and go one way when he's leading me another. Usually missing the Spirit's lead has more to do with my own discomfort than with my lack of discernment. The Spirit wants to lead me into life, but I need to be willing to follow.

That's why I think the main word for Spirit-filled living is this: *surrender.* Mary, the mother-to-be of Jesus, gives us the perfect model of how to surrender to God's Spirit. When she learned that God had chosen her to be the mother of the Messiah, she said, "I am the Lord's servant. May everything you have said about me come true" (Luke 1:38). Other translations simply say, "Let it be done to me as you have said." She surrenders and the Spirit acts. Once again hovering, overshadowing, as he did in Genesis.

But this time rather than bringing order from chaos, the Spirit brings Jesus into the world. And that is what he does still, in your life and in mine. When you open your heart to him and say, "I'm your servant. Let it be done to me as you have said," the Spirit of God produces the life of Jesus in you. You start to care about the things he cares about. You start to love as he loves. Serve as he serves. Think like he thinks, and to feel the love of the Father as he does.

When you feel tired, lifeless, parched for joy . . . Jesus shouts, "Anyone who is thirsty may come to me." He wants to fill you. He wants to give you the life you so desperately need and crave. Because you feel weak, he has promised to send his Spirit. So be filled! Ask him before your feet hit the ground so you can stand your ground. You don't have to live feeling out of breath. The Spirit of God can breathe new life into your heart.

And that's a promise.

CHAPTER 4

BOOMERANG YOUR BLESSINGS

We all have desires and hungers. We all want to feel "full" but so seldom get there. With two teenagers in my house, I'm keenly aware of this hunger because there never seems to be enough food, at least according to my kids. For my son especially, who was bigger and taller than me by thirteen—yes, *thirteen*!—the constant refrain is, "There's nothing to eat!"

It's actually funny, considering that our pantry never goes bare, even if the constants are canned items like pinto beans, fruit, and stewed tomatoes. My son wasn't starving. What he meant was that we were out of mac n' cheese and tortellini, Cap'n Crunch and frozen pizzas. But as soon as we get more, we are out again. One large pizza is not enough unless it's all for him. An eight-pack of tacos? Better get two.

"I've only been full *five* times in my entire life!" he said recently. Apparently, there's not enough tortellini in the world for him to push back from the table and say, "Enough." He's constantly hungry for more no matter how much he has recently consumed.

These "not enough" moments also happen in other areas of life, like finances. Think about the last time you checked the ATM or balanced your checkbook. Did you marvel at how much you have, or did you struggle to cover all your obligations? Or how about your job? Do you come home each day amazed at how energized and appreciated you are? Or does it feel like you barely have the strength to return the next day? How about your time? Do you look at the calendar and wonder what to do with all that free time? Or do you wonder how you'll get it all done?

These are not-enough moments. Not enough money. Not enough time. Not enough energy, patience, connection, happiness, joy, or peace. No matter what you have, you need more of it. And no matter how much more of it you get, it's still never enough. Over time this wears you out and stirs you up. You start to fight to get more of what you need and keep the little you have.

Psychologists and economists call this a "scarcity mentality." It's the idea that resources are limited, so you better get yours—now. It leads to competition, stress, envy, and all kinds of other bad juju. Worst of all, it makes good-hearted people stingy. It's nearly impossible to share what you have when you're constantly worried that you don't have enough. You filter everything through this sense of scarcity, and this mentality destroys generosity, contentment, and gratitude. It makes you live a smaller and smaller life, trying to squeeze ever-diminishing amounts of happiness out of ever-dwindling resources.

Mostly it makes you feel alone.

No one is looking out for you.

So you better look out for yourself.

HALF-FULL OR HALF-EMPTY

Thankfully, there's another way of seeing life—with an abundance mindset. It declares that there will always be more than enough, no matter how much life requires. It's the idea that generosity is hard-wired into reality. I need to breathe, and there is fresh oxygenated air all around me. I need water, and it falls from the sky or comes from the tap. I need gravity, sunlight, food, shelter . . . and all of those things are provided. Even deeper things like community, wisdom, purpose, intimacy, and meaning are available; I just need to access them.

One could say that this is blind optimism. There are plenty of examples of people not getting the basics of life, but before you dismiss the abundance mindset, consider that it's based on the very character of God. God is the source of everything good in this world. He is the Good Shepherd. He loves to see his people well-cared for. There is no scarcity with him because God has no needs yet supplies all. Whenever you see God show up in the Bible, it's so often to bless people—to provide them with what they need, often to a point of overflowing, so that they can in turn be a blessing to others.

As people, we struggle with having enough. We need

help, so God has given us not only the promise of his presence and the promise of life without condemnation. He has not only provided us with his Spirit to guide and direct us. He's also given us the promise: *I will bless you.* We need this blessing to live the life he calls us to lead because without it, we will never have enough, do enough, or be enough. God's blessings are the only cure for not-enough-itis.

And his promise to bless us is likely to be the one that's most misused and misunderstood.

PRESENT TO BLESS

For years, I've wrestled with the belief that God was disappointed in me, that his primary posture towards me was "no." I projected my own insecurities and upbringing onto God, but as I began to dig into the Bible, this perception of God was challenged. I saw a God who loves to bless his people—who delights in pouring out spiritual and physical blessings that empower people to enjoy him and live for his glory. Anytime he said "no," it was to protect some greater "yes." He is not a cosmic killjoy but a loving parent protecting me from things that want to steal my joy.

I was shocked to discover that where God is said to be present in the Bible, his purpose is usually not to judge or correct, but to supply some need. Theologian Wayne Grudem concludes, "When the Bible says that God is 'present' it *usually* means 'present to bless.' The vast majority of biblical references to God's presence are simply more brief ways of stating that he is *present to bless*."[15] When God shows up in people's lives, it's more likely to say "yes" to your need than to say "no" to your requests.

The most powerful proof of God's desire and promise to bless is seen in Jesus. His longest sermon in the Gospels begins with the Beatitudes, which is basically an invitation to blessedness. Think about that. When God comes to earth as a man, his first extended message begins not as a list of all the things you've done wrong but with what the blessed life looks like. He wants to bless you! He came to meet your needs. He came to set things right. Jesus says "yes" to blessing and in him all God's promises are "yes" (see 2 Corinthians 1:20).

It may be hard for us to grasp what "blessing" actually implies. Too often I'm afraid, many people assume God's blessings are given out like a genie's wishes from Aladdin's lamp or like some divine vending machine. At its worst, some people try to "name it and claim it" and make God's favor and blessings into only material wealth and tangible possessions. And it's not that God doesn't bless us materially, but he gives us so much more!

Part of the problem is that outside of church, we don't use the word "bless" as much anymore. You're most likely to roll it out when someone sneezes, which is weird when you think about how gross a sneeze is. In fact, this custom was one I had to learn as an adult. Shortly after I began to date Lori, she sneezed. I just sat there staring into space. She was bothered and asked, "Aren't you going to say, 'Bless you'?"

"Uh, no," I said. "Why should I?" I grew up in house where you didn't say anything when someone sneezed. You left the room to avoid infection and came back to overspray with disinfectant.

She replied, "When you say, 'Bless you,' you're showing attention, care, and simply being polite."

I was amazed. "You get all that from 'Bless you'?"

She did and she says it everywhere. A person can be sitting across a restaurant and if she hears them sneeze, she hollers, "Bless you!" It's a drive-by blessing. I now do it habitually whenever someone sneezes, but I still keep the Purell handy.

Other than after another's sneeze, the word "blessed" is just a new way of saying "lucky" according to linguist Deborah Tannen.[16] I also recall the way my mom used to say, "Bless your heart," which in Texas basically implied that someone was not too smart.

What does the Bible mean when it talks of God's blessing? Surprisingly enough, bless is a relational word. Something is exchanged between two parties, a greater and a lesser. When God is the one blessing, it means to have his favor and power working in your life so that you experience more purpose, peace, and happiness. Bless is also a forward-looking word. It implies God's favor is going to secure a bigger, brighter future.

IN THE BEGINNING

In the opening pages of Genesis, we read that the very first thing God does after creating the man and the woman is to bless them. His first instinct is to bless. As we read on, the entire Bible is filled with God blessing his people. The word actually appears more than 400 times in the Bible with more occurrences in Genesis than any other book.[17] From his first act after humanity's creation and through the sheer number of times "bless" is used in the Bible's first book, God introduces himself as the God who blesses.

These blessings come in a wide variety. God blesses his people to have children, to enjoy food and water, and to have dominion over the earth. He blesses people with his favor, peace, and protection. He showers his blessing on towns and fields, children and crops, breadboards and fruit baskets, harvests of grain and new wine. He blesses with the kingdom of heaven, satisfaction, mercy, the crown of life and every spiritual blessing including his love, adoption, and forgiveness.

These many blessings fit into a few broad categories. The first is a blessing of *productivity*. God supernaturally causes an increase in offspring, wealth, and success. The word "multiply" is frequently used to describe what God promises to do. He accomplishes this, at least partially, by watching over whatever you are trying to produce. When a person grew crops, one of the most feared events was a swarm of locusts. Within a short time, they could eat every green thing, leaving you essentially bankrupt, or your grapes could be hit with disease and rot before they ripened. God's blessing meant he would see to it that these catastrophes don't happen.

Another category of blessing is *protection*. This means that God will keep your enemies at bay, or fight them off himself, often with little effort on your part. One blessing declares that an enemy will attack from one direction and scatter in seven, thanks to God's protection.

A third way God blesses is through *prominence*. The Bible is filled with people who are given positions of great authority, or blessed with good standing among their neighbors. God blessed Joseph to "succeed in all he did," and he ended up the number two leader in Egypt. Nehemiah and Daniel are given similar positions of authority. Solomon's crowning achievement was that other rulers sought him out for wisdom, even paying for the privilege to do so. God's blessing led to prominence and success.

God blesses with *provision*. Whether it be the garden of Eden, the Israelites wandering in the wilderness, or the people living in the Promised Land, God promises to provide. He not only gives a good land, he fills it with good things. Usually, the tougher the situation the more miraculous the way in which he provides. The wandering Hebrews were blessed with a miraculous "bread from heaven," called manna, which appeared each morning. Later, when they had farms, the Lord sent rain "in season," meaning when it was needed most. When God provides, he does it in a way that maximizes the yield.

God also blesses with *purpose*. We see this in the beginning when God not only gives the first humans a wonderful place to live but also a task: to fill and rule the earth. God placed his own image upon them and wanted that image to spread across the world. Even after the fall, we see this recurring theme. God does not just save people from their past, he saves them into a greater future. He calls them to represent his image, to once again be a part of his redemptive work in the world. He blesses with purpose.

We see all these categories of blessing represented in one of the most important biblical promises in the call of Abraham. God says, "Leave your native country, your relatives, and your father's family, and go to the land that I will show you (*provision*). I will make you into a great nation (*productivity*). I will bless you and make you famous, and you will be a blessing to others (*prominence*). I will bless those who bless you and curse those who treat you with contempt (*protection*). All the families on earth will be blessed through you (*purpose*)" (Genesis 12:1–3).

In the New Testament, Paul says that through faith in Jesus, God's promise to Abraham is passed on to you (see Galatians 3:9). You, too, can be blessed with productivity, protection, prominence, provision, and purpose. As with Abraham, these benefits are not supposed to end with you. You are called to pass on these blessing to others. You are granted God's favor to represent his image.

You are blessed to be a blessing.

#BLESSED

People sometimes tag their Twitter posts with #blessed. Often, this comes across as a humble brag. As in, "Just got the keys to my new Rover #blessed" or "Honored to be named top salesperson of the year #blessed." It can all start to feel a little smug and falsely modest. Sensing the irony of some of these posts, comedian Davon Magwood tweeted, "Caught a piece of bacon falling out of my sandwich right before it hit the ground! #blessed."

If God promises to bless his people and care for them, then why do so many not feel #blessed? Again, the biggest error we can slip into is to only equate God's favor with material blessing as if being blessed means nothing more than being rich financially. Our financial lives are important. God can, and does, bless his people materially, but many of us spend our entire lives trying to *get* rich and never stop to consider how to *be* rich. We focus so much on achieving an ever-increasing standard of living that we never realize when, in fact, we have enough.

The progressive nature of Biblical revelation is important here. In the Old Testament, the blessings of God are more rooted in the material: land, rain, rich harvests, silver and gold. It mostly concerns a physical people (the Hebrews) in a physical kingdom (Israel).

As you move into the New Testament, and as God's revelation of himself becomes clearer in Jesus, you find less emphasis on temporary, material blessings and more on eternal, spiritual blessings. The kingdom Jesus builds is not physical, but spiritual; therefore, the blessings he gives are also spiritual. This is not to say that material things no longer matter. Jesus himself says that God will provide for your material needs as you seek him. God's blessings do not diminish; they grow. They now take on a higher and more eternal significance. Material blessings can be enjoyable, but you are also offered the greater gifts of love, joy, forgiveness, and fellowship with God.

Paul explodes with praise in the opening of his letter

to the Ephesians, saying, "All praise to God, the Father of our Lord Jesus Christ, who has *blessed us with every spiritual blessing* in the heavenly realms because we are united with Christ" (Ephesians 1:3, emphasis added). You have every spiritual blessing because you are united with Christ.

A HEAP OF BLESSINGS

What are some of these blessings Paul refers to? He goes on to list many of them in the verses following his opening greeting in Ephesians. For starters, you're blessed with *adoption* as God's children. No longer are you a spiritual orphan scrounging around on your own. There is no more going to bed in fear, not knowing where your next meal will come from, or what could happen while you sleep. You have been adopted into a loving family with a good father. He will provide and take care of you in every way. You're God's kid.

You're blessed with *forgiveness.* Sin is not the end. Through faith in Christ you have "the forgiveness of sins, in accordance with the riches of grace that he lavished on us" (Ephesians 1:7, NIV). Everything you have done and will do is forgiven in Christ. All of it is by his grace.

You're blessed to know the *mystery of God.* This mystery is that God will bring everything together under Christ at the appropriate time. He is working for good in your life and for good in the world. He is bringing his plan to fruition, and you have been marked by the seal of the Holy Spirit in your heart, the guarantee of your inheritance.

You are blessed with *faith.* No matter what happens, you

can look to the future with trust. God has moved in your life remarkably, and he will continue to do so. Paul writes, "And this same God who takes care of me will supply all your needs from his glorious riches, which have been given to us in Christ Jesus" (Philippians 4:19). God supplies you according to his riches. If someone is just above the poverty line and they supply you according to their riches, then you know it won't be much. But God's riches—spiritual, physical, and emotional—are endless. He's got everything in his hands, and *according* to these riches, he'll take care of you. He is rich with everything you need to thrive. You can live each day in faith that God will provide.

You are blessed with *hope.* You are rich in hope because God has prepared a place for you in heaven. It isn't a boring place where people play the harp all day and sit around on clouds with halos. This place is a marvelous new heaven and earth; a place where you will grow, develop, and learn; a space with no more crying, dying, or pain; a place filled with God's presence. Heaven is everything good and wonderful, minus sin and suffering, all raised to the power of God. Words cannot describe what it will be like, but the promise is that it will be better than any human imagination can conceive. So no matter how awesome a place you can imagine, that image does not come close.

Often the very things you long for are the things that God has *already* richly provided for you. You long for love and, "He has given us the Holy Spirit to fill our hearts with his love" (Romans 5:5). You desire peace, and Jesus says, "I am leaving you with a gift—peace of mind and heart" (John

14:27). You search for joy; Jesus says, "I have told you these things so that you will be filled with my joy. Yes, your joy will overflow!" (John 15:11). You need strength: "I can do everything through Christ, who gives me strength" (Philippians 4:13). You need power: "By his divine power, God has given us everything we need for living a godly life" (2 Peter 1:3).

It is not that God *will* give you what you need, but that He *already* has given you all you need. He has *already* blessed you with every spiritual blessing. God blessed you because it brought him "great pleasure" (Ephesians 1:5). He enjoys pouring his blessing into your life. Generosity really is hardwired into the universe. God is the Great Giver and sharing these blessings gives him great pleasure. He loves to bless. You are blessed beyond measure with what he has already done for you.

UNLOCK GOD'S BLESSING

So how can you position yourself for more of God's favor and blessing? Jesus gives some insight when he says, "If you are faithful in little things, you will be faithful in large ones" (Luke 16:10). God watches to see if you're faithful with your little, so you can be trusted with his more.

The word "little" can mean smallest or least significant. Sometimes that's how you may feel. You look at your time and energy, and there's just so little of it. So many people ask you to do so many things. At the end of the day you barely have the energy to crawl into bed so that you can wake up and do it again. You look at your job and think it's so small and insignificant. You wish you could do bigger and better things, but the tasks seem so unimportant. Or maybe you wish you had a life full of friendships and romance, but all you have is a family that drives you crazy.

I don't know what your little is. All I know is that God blesses faithfulness. This means you can stop being frustrated by what you don't have and start being faithful with what you do have. Take a small portion of the time and energy God gives you, and invest it in prayer, reading his Word, and serving others. Do it every day, and soon you'll have more time and energy for the bigger things God provides. Perform your insignificant job like it's the most important role in the world. Do it day after day, and new opportunities will open up. Love and value the people God has already given you, even if they drive you crazy, and you'll find more and better relationships flow into your life. Faithfulness aligns you for more favor. Care for the small things like they're big, and soon God will give you bigger things.

Simply put, obedience positions you for greater blessing. Jesus said, "But even more blessed are all who hear the word of God and put it into practice" (Luke 11:28). When you let go of a grudge, you find freedom on the other side and open yourself to more of God's blessing. When you face a temptation and resist, you show yourself as one who can be trusted with more.

None of us obey perfectly, not even close. Still, obedience is the way you please God and receive his blessing. When you renew your minds with his Word, keep a pure heart, honor your parents, pray for your leaders, do good for others, take care of the poor, and seek holiness, you lay the groundwork for future blessing. Peter says that obedience leads you to enjoy life, see happy days, and it opens God's ears to your prayers (see 1 Peter 3:10–12). John says, "We will receive from him whatever we ask because we *obey* him and do the things that *please* him" (1 John 3:22, emphasis added). More blessings come to those who obey.

A final way you unlock more of God's blessings is to pass them on. After all, the point of receiving God's favor is to bless others. God wants to bless the world by blessing you, and then to bless you more as you bless the world.

BRIDGES OF BLESSING

As a kid, I always thought boomerangs were cool. I mean, it's a stick you can throw as hard as you want and it always comes back—at least if you know what you're doing.

Some people think the boomerang was invented to hunt birds. You'd throw it way out beyond some trees or bushes and as it passes behind them, the boomerang scares the birds out of hiding. In their panic, the birds fly right into the net you've set up. Then, in most studly fashion, you catch the returning boomerang in one hand and cook dinner.

The picture of a boomerang going out and returning with more is an image of blessing. When you're generous with what God has given you, you throw that gift into the world, and it boomerangs back to you as something more. You see this in God's promise to Abraham: "I will bless you and make you famous, and you will be a blessing to others . . . All the families on earth will be blessed through you" (Genesis 12:2–3). God's blessing to Abraham and to the Israelite nation was meant to spread to the world. God's blessing isn't a dead end but a bridge to provide a way for others. Everything you receive from God and pass along generously gets enhanced. You experience more joy, the joy of being generous, and you receive more blessing from God to bless others with. This is the double blessing.

Jesus put it this way: "Give away your life; you'll find life given back, but not merely given back—given back with bonus and blessing. Giving, not getting, is the way" (see Luke 6:37). Blessing grows as you give it away.

This truth flies in the face of modern culture. Our broken answer to happiness almost always revolves around *getting more*. We think it's all about attaining what we don't have and experiencing more and more pleasure and adventure. But God's answer to happiness is not to get more; it's to become more by *giving more*. This principle initiates what we might call the cycle of blessing. As you give, God blesses so that you can give more. Paul points to this cycle when he says, "Yes, you will be enriched in every way so that you can always be generous" (2 Corinthians 9:11). There's a chance that the reason you don't feel very enriched is because generosity is not a priority in your life.

The cycle of blessing is not just about money. Jesus applies this same principle to forgiveness (Luke 6:37). Just as you're called to give money to people who can't pay you back, you're called to give grace and forgiveness to those who don't deserve it. If you're stingy with your forgiveness, your heart begins to shrink. If you forgive quickly and often, your relationships grow and deepen—your gift returns to you with more. If you don't offer grace to those that need it, grace loses significance in your world. If you are full of grace, your world expands, and that gift returns to you as more.

It's not so much a step-by-step formula as it is a description of reality. When you give, more is given to you; so don't withhold your gifts. Don't hold back your love, grace, and forgiveness. Release it. Send it out into the world so God can bless it, and in his timing, boomerang it back to you. When it returns, it will leave you with more than what you started with.

What has God enriched you with? Are you rich with personality? Can you talk for hours and never get tired? Maybe God has blessed you to be a blessing to others who are lonely and need encouragement.

Are you rich with time? Are you at a place in your life where the kids are busy, your spouse is busy and many days it's just you and the dog and a book? Maybe that gift of time is for someone else, like a single mom who needs a few hours to herself or a kid who needs a father figure.

Are you rich with energy? You never stop moving and shaking. From morning 'till night you are on. Let me tell you who needs that energy . . . your church's children's and student ministries!

God has enriched you with something. You have something extra to pass on to others. You have been blessed to be a blessing to others. It takes an act of faith to give when you feel like you have little, but here is what you'll find: when you're generous *with* your life, God is generous *in* your life. You do not become more by getting more; you give more to become more. You can double your blessing.

THE VALLEY OF BLESSING

Sometimes in the tough season, in the valley, God is preparing to bless you. A powerful reminder of this truth is found in a scene from King Jehoshaphat's life. The surrounding nations had declared war on Judah. The situation looked impossible and their destruction appeared inevitable. In fear, Jehoshaphat cried out to God and ordered the people to fast. He prayed publically with great humility and dependence on God.

God's spirit came upon a man named Jahaziel, and he challenged them to head out the next day for the battle: "But you will not even need to fight. Take your positions; then stand still and watch the Lord's victory" (2 Chronicles 20:17). The next day they prepared to head out for battle and Jehoshaphat reminded them to stand firm and believe, "and you will succeed" (20:20).

Their battle plan was strange. They sent the worship team out ahead of the army to praise and sing to God. Could there be a more ridiculous sight? Here is an army being led by musicians—not warriors—yet as the musicians sang, the armies they approached were thrown into confusion. They turned on each other and started to fight amongst themselves. They literally destroyed each other.

By the time Jehoshaphat's scouts got to the lookout point, they saw bodies everywhere. The battle had already been won. The opposing armies had wiped each other out. There was so much plunder, clothes, and supplies that it took them three days to collect it all.

Then something very significant happened. Jehoshaphat got everyone together in the valley near where the battle took place. They praised God and thanked him. They did not forget the Giver of the gifts in the middle of the valley. And the valley was named, "The Valley of Blessing"—the valley where God blessed his people and his people blessed him back. God took an impossible situation and turned it into a miraculous opportunity.

God turns the valley of the shadow of death into the valley of blessing. He turns dark nights into moments where his light breaks through. He blesses in the tough places and the hopeless circumstances where only he can achieve the victory. It doesn't usually happen when we want it to happen or how we think it should happen, but God loves to do the impossible.

If you're in the valley, take courage. If there doesn't appear to be enough, cry out to God and depend on him. Trust God to fight for you. Believe the battle is already won. Your valley is God's opportunity to show you blessing.

God has promised to bless you. He will meet all your material and spiritual needs so that you can bless others. Thank him for all he's done and all he's about to do. Then stand and watch as God transforms the valley of your struggle into the peak of his blessings.

The promise of his blessings releases you to enjoy life to the fullest.

CHAPTER 5

A NEW MIXTAPE

Many people remain caged not by circumstances but by old labels about who they are. Instead of living in the promise of having a new identity in Christ and the liberation this promise brings, they remain trapped by false messages, past mistakes, and old voices. Together, these create a chorus of lies constantly echoing through their minds.

It reminds me of the old mixtapes I used to make as a teenager. Before CDs and mp3s, the music world of the 1980s was dominated by cassette tapes. These small rectangular devices were more portable than eight-track tapes and more durable than vinyl. If they didn't sound amazing, none of us knew the difference. We'd seen the commercial of a guy in a lounge chair whose hair was blown back by the clarity and volume of a cassette. Plus, cassettes were in "hi-fidelity." Whatever that meant, it sounded cool and promised the best listening experience possible.

I had a huge boombox with two cassette decks, powered by enough D batteries to make lifting it qualify for a P90X workout. I loved my boombox, but the Walkman portable cassette player with headphones changed my life. I still remember where I was the first time I listened to a Walkman: the middle school cafeteria in the mid-eighties. The song was "Juke Box Hero" by *Foreigner.* (I can't remember my driver's license number, but I remember that first song on a Walkman). Cassettes were the bomb, and I had hundreds of them before CDs eclipsed them and before digital swallowed all predecessors.

To maximize my boombox and Walkman, I spent untold hours creating mixtapes, basically the precursor to the digital playlist, only more difficult and time consuming. Back then, there was no dropping and dragging songs into a playlist in seconds. To compile a mixtape took the talent of an artist and the patience of a saint. (I feel like a grandpa here: "Listen kids, we also walked to school uphill both ways, barefoot if we were lucky. Otherwise, we rode a packed-out school bus with mean high-schoolers before anti-bullying was a thing!")

Here's the scientifically-engineered process for making a mixtape: You cue up a favorite song from one cassette deck and hit pause. You set up the other deck with your Memorex or Maxwell master blank cassette and hit both pause and record. Then at the same time you release both pause buttons, and play the song from one cassette while recording it to another. After this is accomplished, you must expertly pause the blank cassette. Then you'd go searching for another cassette for a different song. You'd fast-forward and rewind until the song was teed up perfectly and then you'd record that song to the master tape. I wasn't making amateur mixtapes, people. This creative process would take days or even whole weeks for a two-sided mixtape.

Why go to all the trouble? Often it was for a special someone. You'd get it all done and then rock up to middle school, find the person you really liked, and hand it to them as cool as ice: "Hey, I made you a mixtape. No biggie, see ya." Game on.

HEARING VOICES

While cassette mixtapes are as obsolete as rotary phones and fax machines, you still have a mixtape that plays in your mind every day. Instead of Foreigner, Journey, or Run—D.M.C., your mixtape often plays back negative and destructive messages you've recorded from assorted sources—parents, friends, media, culture, students, enemies, bullies, teachers, and exes. It plays the hurts you've experienced and the wounds you carry and the echoes of past put-downs and devastating confrontations.

We each have our custom-made, sure-to-hit-us-where-it-hurts mix, but maybe yours sounds something like this: *You're nobody. Nobody! You'll never amount to anything. You'll never succeed. People don't like you. You'll always be ugly. You'll never be enough. You're just a jock or a nerd, a clown or a geek; a gamer, joker, stoner, pretty face, foreigner, slacker, gym-rat, egghead, whore, dropout, druggie, ghetto kid, punk, depressed, trailer trash, hood, hippie, troublemaker, mixed, black, brown, or white bum. You're too fat or too skinny. You're weird. You're no good. You're stupid. You're just like your mother or father. You'll never break through. Nobody will listen to you. Nobody will ever love you. Things will never change. You deserve abuse. You've always been this way.*

This old, worn-out mixtape reinforces your old identity in powerful and destructive ways. It keeps you trapped in lies and prevents you from fully embracing your new identity. It straps you to a defeated vision of yourself, like the restraints that hold down a death-row inmate before lethal injection. But the beautiful and freeing reality is that through faith in Christ those restraints are already loosed. They only have the power you choose to give them. You can rise up in faith and walk in a new life. To do this, you must habitually and consistently record over that old mixtape with the new mixtape that God provides.

There's a much better soundtrack for your life if you're willing to shred the old mixtape. Paul reminds us of how God sees us: "I'll call nobodies and make them somebodies; I'll call the unloved and make them beloved. In the place where they yelled out, 'You're nobody!' they're calling you 'God's living children'" (Romans 9:25–26, MSG). This is God's promise: *I will give you a new identity.* We go from nobody to somebody, from unloved to loved. This truth is the better mixtape—the one you must listen to over and over to be brave and free.

Each of God's promises that we have considered—his

presence, his work of freedom and salvation in our lives, his Spirit, and his many blessings—all lead to you living out of a new identity. This identity operates from a place of freedom and security that God's presence provides. It impacts everything you do, and this promise has the power to fundamentally change how you relate to yourself, to God, and to others.

TRADING NAMES

Have you ever wished you could change your name? You know, take on a name less common or take a more common one if you are tired of spelling your uncommon name out, like me? Some people have gone so far as to legally change their name but not always for the better. *Huffington Post* reported on some extreme name changers. Tyler Gold, a young entrepreneur, changed his legal name to: Tyrannosaurus Rex Joseph Gold. He did this because it "sounds cooler." Trust me, it won't sound cooler to his future teenager! [18]

Scott Edwards Knoll changed his name on his 30th birthday to "Optimus Prime," a nod to the movie *Transformers,* which could be confused for an improved version of Amazon Prime. As a teenager, George Garrett changed his name to "Captain Fantastic Faster than Superman, Spiderman, Batman, Wolverine, the Hulk, and the Flash combined." No lie. He may have the world's longest name, but his grandmother won't speak to him anymore.

The desire for a name change gets to your identity because names are a part of who you are. Names are how people identify you and think of you. It seems that no matter where you turn, people are trying to define you. There are all kinds of articles about how your cars or pets or even your likes and follows on social media define you. Other people tell you who you are through their expectations and labels. They call you the crazy friend or the one who's always there. You're the good kid or the kid that never quite lives up to expectations. You're the person who always gets the job done or the one who is always overlooked.

You tend to live up (or down) to other's expectations, or you go the other direction and rebel against what people expect. In either case, you draw much of your identity from other people—and that is a shaky place to live because people are messed up. I'm messed up. You're messed up. Even the people you look up to are messed up. People are often selfish and inconsistent, which means your identity can never be solid if you base it on how others *feel* about you.

This measure of identity is nothing new. Ancient thinkers warned of tying your value to public opinion. The Greek philosopher Plato used a powerful image to describe those who courted public opinion. He said they were like people "keeping a monster." Imagine yourself chained to a violent, hungry beast. If you don't keep it happy and well-fed, it will turn on you, tear you to pieces, and eat you as its next meal. Not only is this an exhausting life, it begins to fundamentally alter what you think is good and bad, right and wrong. Plato concludes, "Good is what pleases him [the monster], evil what he dislikes; truth and beauty are determined only by the taste of the brute."[19] To get your identity and self-worth from what other people think is a treacherous place to live. It's like being chained to a monster.

Your heart, however, is meant to receive value and identity from a much deeper place than your friends or culture. What others expect isn't nearly as important as what God says about you. He is the only one in your life that truly needs nothing from you but wants everything for you. He does not need to feed on you to get value; he wants to give himself to you so that you can become even more.

You see this reality acted out in a powerful way in the book of Revelation. An angel appears to John in a vision and offers both a challenge and an encouragement. In the vision, the risen Jesus says, "And I will give to each one a white stone, and on the stone will be engraved a new name that no one understands except the one who receives it" (Revelation 2:17). The white stone is a mysterious symbol. Commentators have speculated on what it means for centuries. Some say it represents a not-guilty verdict in a Roman court of law. Others believe it represents a ticket to a feast. Some believe the white stone alludes to the trophies handed out to victorious athletes competing in public games. When they flashed that pebble to people, it not only got them admiration and praise, but it also provided them access to special feasts, free stuff, and unique privileges.

I don't think you have to choose between those meanings. The white stone means you are free, declared righteous, invited into awesomeness as a victorious champion. Those are all facts of your salvation, but don't miss the main point: it is Jesus who grants you this status. He is the one who hands you the stone. This means you are no longer identified by the destructive names you have carried throughout your life. People may have said you are a loser, but Jesus says you share in his victory. Others may have said you aren't worth anything, but Jesus says you're worth dying for. Others claim you will never change or make anything of yourself. Jesus says that your old identity is in the past, and he offers you a new name today. Your name is Accepted. Loved. Overcomer. Victor.

Just reading through the New Testament, you see so many places where you are called out with a new identity. Here's a partial list of the things the New Testament says, "you are," as a person of faith. You are Jesus' followers, Jesus' friends, children of God, children of light, members of God's family, holy and blameless standing before God without a single fault. You are God's people, the salt of the earth, the light of the world, the branches that bear fruit. You are God's field, building, living stones in God's temple, holy priests, a holy nation, a chosen people. You are God's workers, Christ's ambassadors, true ministers of God united with Christ. You are a part of his body living by the Spirit, God's masterpiece, the faithful ones. You are meant for better things, receiving a kingdom that is unshakable, looking forward to a home yet to come. You are heirs of God's glory, set free from slavery to sin. You are truly free!

This is God's mixtape—one he spent untold time on and created in his constant patience and displays of love. One he ultimately demonstrated in the life and death of Jesus. These words are what he desires you to play over the destructive messages of the old mixtape. Play it until that mixtape gets erased and replaced. Play it until it embeds itself deeply in your subconscious. Play it until you live like you believe it.

WAR AND PEACE

The power of words that you speak to yourself and to others are very important parts of embracing this new identity. The words we speak as well as the ones we hear carry incredible weight and power. They can literally make your life one of war and conflict or one of peace and contentment. You shape your words, then your words shape you.

James explains, "We can make a large horse go wherever we want by means of a small bit in its mouth. And a small rudder makes a huge ship turn wherever the pilot chooses to go, even though the winds are strong. In the same way, the tongue is a small thing that makes grand speeches" (James 3:3–4). You may not think about your tongue being such a powerful part of your body, but when you're sick, what's one of the first things the doctor says to you? Stick out your tongue. Your tongue reveals something about what's going on inside of you. James says the tongue is significant because it steers our lives, like a bit in a horse's mouth, or a rudder on a ship. It reveals deep, internal things. If you want to know where you're going to be in the next five to ten years, look at what you said today. Your words are the rudder; they determine the direction. Without a course correction, your words today tell the story of your tomorrow.

Consider the mixtape of what you think and speak.

Maybe you believe your marriage is always going to struggle and never change. Perhaps you believe you'll never find someone to share your life with. Maybe you believe that your job or career is never going to get better. You will always be broke. Your business will never improve. A family member will never get straightened out. You are convinced people cannot change. You tell yourself and close friends these things again and again.

If you believe something long enough, you will likely live in such a way to prove you are right. You replay a destructive belief, speak it, affirm it, and eventually fulfill it. You don't embrace a new identity without a new way of thinking and speaking to yourself and to others. The new beliefs must be reinforced at every turn to take root.

I struggle in this area. At times, the old mixtape loops a few times before I realize I'm listening. At other times, I know which song is playing, and I enjoy wallowing in it, like a sad country song on an otherwise beautiful day. I sing along and deep down something broken in me likes the misery, yet I know this is not the whole truth, not the redemptive message that God sings over me. This is not the song that will raise my vision to God and boldly empower me to embrace his future. So, in my better moments, I stop the tape and remind myself of who God is, of all he has done, can do, and promises to do. I take charge of the words I allow myself to camp out on, and I refuse to limit God.

The next time you say to yourself, "Our marriage will *never* change." Stop. Step back. Check yourself before you wreck yourself. You don't *know* that. You aren't God. You don't speak as God. He can change a heart, a marriage, or a family, and there are thousands of couples who confess he did exactly that. So stop limiting the unlimited God!

When the old mixtape plays, "I'll *always* be broke. I'll never have enough." Press pause. You don't know the future. You can't even control what happens in the next hour. Remind yourself that no matter what you have, it is enough because God is enough. Be faithful in the little until God brings the more.

The next time you hear, "My son or daughter won't change—it's *impossible*. People don't change." Take out the tape. That is a lie from the pit of hell! God has changed millions and millions of people. I'm one of them. So are you. Don't write somebody off that God can write in, which is everybody and anybody.

When the old internal voice shouts, "You're nobody," stand on God's Word: "I'll call nobodies and make them somebodies" (Romans 9:25, MSG). God is the one whose opinion ultimately counts—more than yours or your neighbors. Believe you are somebody in him because the consequences of believing you're a nobody are disastrous.

If you believe you are a nobody, you start to parent like a nobody. This belief gets transferred to your kids in all kinds of unhealthy ways. You interact with your spouse from a broken place of self-loathing and your marriage suffers. You interact at work from insecurity and your confidence spikes up and down like an out of control EKG. Studies show that people treat you how you give them permission to treat you. Believe you're a nobody and people will eventually treat you accordingly.

But if you believe you are somebody in God, you parent from a place of value. Your kids see a model for one who holds their head high with significance. You work from a place of confidence and trust in God and boldly take risks and press forward. You love your spouse and family from a grounded self-worth based in God's worth, which empowers them to be all God made them to be.

This isn't pride but a humble posture that realizes I was a nobody, but God made me a somebody—thanks be to God! Pride wants to be better than others. Aspiration wants to be the best version of yourself. Aspire to be all that God has made you to be, and don't compare yourself to others. The greatest gift you can give is your true, God-empowered self—the somebody he is making you into, the special person he created you to be.

You may still have days where you feel like a nobody, where the old mixtape plays on relentlessly, but God says you are somebody. You don't need any more followers on social media to matter. You don't need to look a certain way, have a six-pack (thank God!), or lose weight to have worth. You don't need any more accomplishments, degrees, promotions, or acceptance to be praiseworthy. You don't need to drive a nicer car, live in a bigger house, or have more money to count. In fact, if you make your value dependent on others' opinions of you, you will never fully rest in the value you already have. When you live this way, the monster inside will always want more.

No matter what you've been through, what others have

told you, or what you still battle telling yourself, you must cling to your true, God-given identity. Your old mixtape doesn't have the power to keep you caged—unless you let it.

HIDDEN WITH CHRIST

I recently encountered a unique strategy for dealing with the critical voices that enter my life. The source was a bright, young philosopher named Taylor Swift. In one of her best-known songs, she begins by defining the problem, revealing that no matter what she does, other people are going to talk about her. Her response to this existential conundrum is found in the song's super-catchy chorus that also serves as its title: "Shake It Off."

The wisdom in this song is spot-on.

The world *is* full of players, haters, heartbreakers, and fakers; all kinds of people who will steal your joy and break your heart. They want to tell you who you are. They want to shape you to their own image. They want to steal your identity. Maybe you've allowed others to steal your identity. You've allowed labels to create a veneer over who you really are. You've allowed all kinds of circumstances and situations to rob you of the truth about who God says you are, but it's not too late to reclaim your real identity and live in the fullness of the new person you are in Jesus Christ. You can shake it off.

Remember that in Revelation, Jesus not only hands the victor a stone but that "on the stone will be engraved a *new name* that no one understands except the one who receives it" (2:17). This image gets at one of the most powerful and mysterious aspects of your identity. It's the notion that all you are, and who you are, is hidden in God and kept safe. Not even you know all of who you are—there is more to you than you can imagine.

One day, however, you will stand in front of your Savior and he will tell you your true name. He'll hand it to you, the clouds will clear, and possibly for the first time in your existence you will declare, "Wow! So *that's* who I fully am!" The personal nature of this revelation is found in the phrase that says, "no one understands except the one who receives it." It's the name only you can know. You will finally be whole, complete, and right.

Paul put it this way: "For you died to this life, and your real life is hidden with Christ in God. And when Christ, who is your life, is revealed to the whole world, you will share in all his glory" (Colossians 3:3–4). The real you is hidden in Christ. One day, everyone will see you as you really are, and in the meantime, you have a new life to discover and live out. Like a marathon runner, endurance and direction are the keys to finishing the race. The more you discover Christ, the more you discover yourself. The more you turn away from him, the more you slip away from the identity he keeps for you.

PROTECT YOUR IDENTITY

When Jesus offers the white stones with new names, he reveals two significant identity-stealers: desire and idolatry.

Both have the power to lead you away from your true self and shake up your identity.

After commending the believers in Revelation for staying faithful through a time of persecution, Jesus refers to an iconic Old Testament story (see 2:14). A foreign King, Balak, figured out how to sideline the people of Israel from living in their God-given identity. He realized he could not destroy the Israelites from the outside, so he sought to ruin them from the inside. He helped lure the Israelites into sexual experiences with those who wanted to destroy them. The sex led to idolatry, where the people of God began to bow down and worship false gods. What could not be accomplished by force was accomplished through desire. The people of God trapped themselves by stepping away from their identity.

Identity Thief #1: Desire

The believers in Revelation to which Jesus spoke had withstood the outside pressure of persecution but were giving in to the inside pressures of temptation and desire. They lived in a culture where casual sex was considered a good thing and it was often tied to the public worship of a pagan god. Some went to love feasts where they not only ate meat sacrificed to idols, but they would also visit the temple prostitutes. This behavior was so ingrained in their way of life that people in the church would still participate in these activities and teach others to do so as well, often under the umbrella of grace and forgiveness. They took the idea of liberty and freedom as a follower of Jesus to the extreme.

Jesus gives them a solemn warning. He basically says, "You're about to lose yourself." When you have no boundaries, you are like a home without walls. Eventually there's no difference between the inside and the outside, and you are exposed to harsh elements. When it comes to worship and sex, God has some very clear boundaries meant to protect your new life. These are such powerful experiences that you can easily get lost in them—no matter how casual you think they are—and confuse your identity.

You probably know at least one friend or family member who got wrapped up in a bad romance. While in the throes of love, they simply cannot see that every other area of their life is in decline. They become hostile to family, neglect friends, and ignore the clear signs and evidence that this relationship is not good for them. You say things like, "I feel like I don't even know them anymore. They sound like someone else. They've completely changed." And it's true. Their identity has been hijacked. They are losing themselves in someone else.

The physical act of sex not only fires up the pleasure centers of the brain, it releases a bonding hormone that makes you feel irrationally attached to the other person. Researchers have also found that couples that feel the sensation of "being in love" have reduced blood flow to the portion of their brains that allows them to think critically, and this condition can last up to eighteen months. So while you can treat sex casually, your body does not. The entire physiological process is designed to bond you to the other person. If sexual intimacy is not honored with the right person in the right context of marriage, you will face a gravitational pull away from your new life in Christ.

When I talk to friends who've drifted from the faith and returned, it rarely has to do with a crisis of belief. Often it was a romantic relationship. They got lost in love. Then the love faded, and they stayed lost. This pattern often repeats until they made a choice to agree with God's take on relationships. They paired up with someone who was committed to following Christ, and then honored the physical boundaries. This time around, they not only fell in love, but they didn't drift away and they didn't lose themselves.

If you are in a relationship with someone who is not a Christ follower or who is not as committed as you are, then you know the tension I'm describing. Everything feels tangled and complicated. You feel divided in your loyalty. You might even feel a little sick to your stomach reading this, but take heart. The solution is dangerously simple: raise Christ to the number one position in your heart. He is the one whose love you can always trust. When you make him number one, every other thing in your life begins to line up.

Some tension may linger, but the more you focus on Jesus, the more you will experience his peace—even when tempted. It may feel like losing yourself, but remember: you are only losing a false version of yourself. Your true self is hidden in Christ, not in any other person. His is the only love you can never lose, and the more you give yourself to your Savior, the more you become the person you know you can be. The more you become proud of who you are and what you do. The more you can look at yourself in the mirror and see a brave person looking back.

What this means for you is between you and Jesus. It might mean investing more time in things God is calling you to do. It might mean a change of address, a change of heart, or a change in who you date. It might mean recommitting to a church community. It may mean some time alone to reflect and pray.

No matter how you are led, be sure of this: You are being led right back to the best version of yourself. You are being led to a strong place of freedom. God is in the life changing business, and sometimes change means letting go of the comfortable to embrace the possible. Just be you for a while. Get ready to be delighted in what God reveals when you take him to heart.

Identity Thief #2: Idolatry

The second warning Jesus issues that can steal our identity is in regard to idol worship. You don't see many people worshipping little statues anymore, but there are plenty of idols left in our culture. An idol is something good that we elevate to an ultimate place in our life. Money, power, health, status, reputation, and talent can all become idols that displace God as the one we look to for significance and reward. This struggle means we need to push back on some assumptions in our culture.

Our culture says it's all about survival of the fittest. Our faith says the meek shall inherit the earth. The culture says sexual purity doesn't matter. Our faith says we should honor God with our bodies. The culture says having more is the answer. Our faith says generosity is the answer. The culture says fame, power, and money are the highest goals. Our faith tells us that love is the highest goal. The culture says that if you want it, you have to take it. Our faith says that God will provide it. The culture says that if it feels good, just go and do it. Why? Because YOLO: You only live once. Our faith says, "You may only live once, but you live forever." Make it count in the sense of not only doing what feels good but doing what is good. Honor God with what he's given you.

How do we protect our new identity? We become aware of what we are doing, how we are living, and how we are navigating life. Realize that identity thieves come from without and within. Both desire and idols can lead us into amnesia as it relates to our new identity in Christ. We can forget who we are, but if we walk with our heart toward God and with an awareness of these thieves, we can protect the somebody he's making us into.

I wish I had a foolproof way to always live in this new identity, but it's something I wrestle with continually. I've found that this victory is won in the small things, in tiny acts of faithfulness.

So I remind myself regularly of who God says I am. I press pause on the mixtape of negative thoughts that plays through my mind—often many times a day. I get enough sleep because a worn-out mind produces defeated thoughts and emotions. I keep digging into the Bible, praying my way through different passages. I read a verse, pause and ask God for whatever that text is saying, or I thank God for who he is and what the text says he provides for me. I make time to stimulate my mind intellectually to think about the things of God because this is how I feel close to God.

And I talk to myself. Seriously, I do. I speak God's word over my life, reminding myself of the many promises God makes. I ask God's Spirit to fill me and guide me. I pray for spiritual gifts and for boldness so that I may faithfully carry out my purpose. I ask others to pray for me. I share what I'm learning with my wife or close friends. I don't try to do it alone. Nothing here is new in what I do, but the power is in the habits.

Whatever label you have been carrying around—unwanted, unloved, burden, screw-up, worthless, nobody—Jesus has come to rip away that broken identity and give you a fresh start. You are not unwanted; you are chosen. You are not a burden; you are blessed to be a blessing. You are not a nobody; you are God's somebody. You are not unloved; you are loved. You are God's child by choice! That's the promise God sealed on the cross, and baptism is your new birth certificate. He gave his life to give you a new name.

It's time to dance to his new mixtape.

CHAPTER 6

THE FORBIDDEN RED VELVET CUPCAKE

One of the greatest obstacles to enjoying the uncaged life is our ongoing struggle with temptation. No matter how spiritually mature or devoted we are to following Jesus, as human beings we will always face temptations in this life. Understanding and appropriating God's promises, however, can empower us in this battle. We can accept his grace and the promise of his forgiveness and live in his power to find freedom.

Or we can remain caged in self-condemnation and the consequences of our poor choices.

The choice is ours—and even in simple matters—it's never easy.

TASTE OF TEMPTATION

"*Don't eat my cupcake.*"

It was a simple, clear request. One I repeated no less than three times to my teenage kids. We'd just celebrated our Easter meal at *Red Robin*. How a burger place became our go-to spot for Easter, I can't remember—but yes, it's pretty pathetic.

Technically, it was a few days before Easter. As a pastor I've learned that if we don't celebrate early, I'll be a zombie by Easter afternoon after all of the services. Lori has memories of me in the backyard "hiding" Easter eggs for our kids. I sat in a chair, barely awake, chin on my chest, chucking the eggs all over the yard. That's when she instituted the Wilhite Family Holiday rule. We do our celebrating *before* the church activities when dad is still among the living.

We decided to hit a gourmet cupcake place on the way home. These cupcakes looked amazing. Each kid got to pick out two as an Easter treat. I picked one for myself—a red velvet cupcake with vanilla buttercream icing swirled high on the top, a thing of beauty. Too good to just wolf down, I planned to let my anticipation build and savor this cupcake. I would eat this treat *after* all the Easter services were done, a sweet and delicious sugar bomb to celebrate the Resurrection.

The kids could eat theirs whenever they wanted, but I made it clear, "Nobody eats my cupcake." They agreed. I made them promise. More than once. We got home. I put my cupcake in the fridge and slid it to the back. For the next couple of days, I'd see it every time I grabbed something, smile, and think, "Soon."

Easter services rolled along and we finally got to the last one. Call me shallow, but I began to think about that cupcake. I even had a plan. I would put it in the microwave for ten seconds, just until the icing softened but didn't run down the sides. I planned to kick off my shoes, put my aching feet up, and eat that cupcake bit by bit, savoring every bite, drawing it out as long as possible. I had earned it. This was my reward.

Returning home after church, I went straight to the kitchen and then I saw it: the empty box my cupcake had been in. Red crumbs on the counter. *No—this could not be happening!*

I stormed off to find my kids.

"Do you know where my cupcake is?" I asked the first kid I encountered.

Silence. You know, the guilty kind of silence that speaks volumes.

"You *promised* me you would not eat my cupcake!"

And then, the kid-who-shall-not-be-named said, "Dad, I'm sorry. I guess I have a problem with food. I just couldn't resist it."

All I could do was walk away and vow to find a better hiding place next time.

DON'T TEMPT ME

I couldn't stay frustrated for too long because the truth is, I struggle with temptation in my own life. I've eaten the forbidden red velvet cupcake plenty of times. I have problems with selfishness, pride, anger, and any number of other things. I feel the pull to do stuff I know I shouldn't do. I think thoughts and speak words that are all kinds of wrong. I'm baffled at my own behavior at times. We all are.

Maybe you need to control your temper, stop tearing into people, or blowing up. But then that person starts driving you crazy again, pushing your buttons. You feel your blood boiling, *and you eat the cupcake.* You know that guy or girl is no good for you. You vow, never again. I am not seeing them! Then the phone rings. You get a text. They like your post on social media, and *you eat the cupcake.* You know you should get to church on the weekend, but you're tired. And the game is on, *and you eat the cupcake, and then the pizza.*

These mistakes are what it means to be human. You know what you should do, but you are constantly tempted to cave. Paul bottom lines it for us: "I have discovered this principle of life—that when I want to do what is right, I inevitably do what is wrong" (Romans 7:21). The struggle with temptation is baked right into life. Wanting what's right, but doing what's not right. These failures can lead to feelings of defeat and guilt. You hear that inner voice saying, *And you call yourself a Christian?* You go from feeling bad about what you did to feeling shame about who you are. Your self-worth plummets. You feel like a huge fraud. No wonder Paul exclaims, "What a miserable person I am!" (7:24).

Paul also gives you the ultimate solution to your sin problem: "Thank God! The answer is in Jesus Christ our Lord" (7:25).

Through faith in Jesus, your sin problem is solved: he paid

the ultimate price for the ultimate problem so you could be free from all condemnation. He not only gives the amazing promise of his presence, he backs that promise up by providing your forgiveness, filling you with his Spirit, blessing you with material and spiritual blessings, and offering you a new identity. He has cleared the way for you to walk with God and enjoy his presence as the greatest promise of all.

While the condemnation war is over, the temptation battle rages on.

Our freedom has been won on the cross, but we still struggle to live in that freedom. It's a battle to grow into the person you really are in Christ—the *you* you are called to be, made to be, and meant to be. You don't resist temptation to hang on to your salvation. You resist temptation to grow, thrive, and receive all the good things God wants to give you. You resist to give joy and honor to the One who loved you and gave himself up for you. You resist because you don't want to drift and end up someplace that is no fun to be.

This is why I'm grateful for this epic promise of God: *I will help you stand in temptation*. Paul writes of this promise:

> "If you think you are standing strong, be careful not to fall. The temptations in your life are no different from what others experience. And God is faithful. He will not allow the temptation to be more than you can stand. When you are tempted, he will show you a way out so that you can endure" (1 Corinthians 10:12–13).

God is aware of the temptations you face. I don't believe he leads you to sin, but he does allow temptation and testing. In fact, the term temptation can also be translated "trial." If you face a difficulty and remain faithful, this becomes a trial God uses to grow your faith. If you face a difficulty and resort to sin, the trial becomes a temptation that damages your soul. God sees to it personally that no temptation will be too much to bear. He always shows you a way out. The trick is to take it because you won't always want to.

Especially when someone hurts you.

FOOTHOLDS AND STRONGHOLDS

It was two o'clock in the morning and I couldn't sleep. Lying in bed and staring at the spinning ceiling fan, I found my thoughts circling like the blades above me. I replayed the events of the day over and over.

I couldn't believe someone I considered a friend had gone behind my back for months and violated my trust. Totally betrayed and I never saw it coming. All night, the questions ran through my mind: "How could he do this? Why would he do this? What did I ever do to him? Why didn't I see this coming? And how am I, as a pastor who should set an example, supposed to respond?"

My frustration and hurt simmered into anger. I began to imagine ways of dealing back some of the pain he had dealt to me—little things I could say, subtle actions I could take. I clearly had the higher ground. I was in the right. I was the injured party.

My anger felt good and fueled the various methods of retaliation that I continued to imagine. It felt righteous and comfortable. It was power . . . and I liked it. As I held on to those angry thoughts, they quickly began to hold on to me. And even though I didn't feel it at the time, a seed of bitterness took root in my heart, and the temptation to water it felt irresistible.

At the same time another voice rose up—a nagging unwelcome voice. It reminded me of Ephesians 4:27 and a little word picture that says, "Anger gives a foothold to the devil." I knew what this meant. I had taught it and spoken about it. It meant that anger is like the tiny cracks and imperfections in a rock face. They give a little place to plant your foot. Give a mountain climber a foothold, and he'll use it to climb even higher. Anger gives the devil that kind of leverage—a way to climb into your heart.

This reminder pointed to a way out in letting go of the anger, but in that moment, it demanded that I let go of my right to be hurt, my right to be offended. To be honest, it felt a little like dying, like letting go of the only thing that felt right in a raging sea of wrong.

All of this banged around in my head through my sleepless night. In the morning, I realized I had already given in to temptation. I had started down a road that would never end in freedom. I looked at my disheveled self in the bathroom mirror, bags under my bloodshot eyes from lack of sleep, crazy hair, and said, "No."

No, I would not give the devil a foothold into my heart. I would forgive. I would let go of my right to get even and give this situation to God. I would climb down off my pedestal of victimhood and remember I'd done far worse and God has forgiven me. I would fight to live in the freedom God offers me. I was offered a way out and I took it. I don't always.

The fight was not won that morning. It was only the beginning, but it's a fight worth having. Unforgiveness is one of the most subtle and deadly temptations you will face. The devil wants a secure place in your life from which to operate. His strategy is to turn footholds into strongholds.

A foothold of anger eventually becomes a stronghold of bitterness. Your heart gets closed off to others. You stop trusting. You become cynical and lose faith in what God can do. You brood more, smile less, and stop living in hope. All the while you become less effective, more self-focused, and more self-reliant. It is heavy. And it's deadly. Hold grudges long enough and they start to hold you.

The only way out of the stronghold of bitterness is forgiveness. I've found forgiveness is not a once-and-done thing. It's a process, a continual releasing of grievance. One thing that helps me most is praying for that other person. The first prayer might be short. Something like, "Help that jerk." You won't feel it, but you said it. Eventually you can pray something like, "Protect their family." Your heart softens over time, and you graduate to, "God, show up in their life. Bless them. Help them feel your love." Each time you pray, the stronghold of bitterness crumbles, and one day it's gone.

Grace can grab a foothold, too. Take the way out. Forgive to be free. Acknowledge the temptations you are up against and lean in to God for strength and favor to overcome them.

PRIVATE LOGIC

The main problem with temptation is not its badness but its goodness. It often offers something legitimately desirable, but in an illegitimate way. Intimacy is good, but an affair is bad. Money is good, but stealing it is bad. Justice is good; revenge is bad. This may seem oversimplified but nonetheless true. While temptation may feel right in one way, it's wrong in so many others. And the enemy knows how to find your weak spots and blindside you with just the very thing you think you need: love, comfort, success, provision, confidence, pleasure—the list goes on and on.

So how can you be proactive in protecting yourself in the midst of temptation? One of the best ways is to know yourself and recognize your private logic, which is what I call the central operating system of your identity. Private logic guides your thoughts and actions and develops over your whole life as you consciously and subconsciously answer these three essential questions:

1. *What kind of person am I?*
2. *What kind of world do I live in?*
3. *Knowing the kind of person I am, how can I get what I want and need in a world like this?*

Resisting temptation starts with clarifying these questions and hanging on to your answers through faith. *Who am I?* A child of God—one filled with God's Spirit and set apart to live from an amazing new identity. *What kind of world do I live in?* One with a loving Father who is making all things new, including myself. *What would a person like me do to get what I want and need in a world like this?* Pray, wait, trust, and obey.

Temptation strikes by challenging the first two questions. It presents you with something you want while subtly challenging your world and identity. You can see the process at work in the very first temptation recorded in the Bible.

When the serpent arrives in Genesis, his first question to Eve is, "Did God really say you must not eat the fruit from any of the trees in the garden?" (Genesis 3:1). He's asking how a person like her gets what she wants in a world like Eden. There's already a subtle insinuation she *cannot* get what she needs. The serpent questions whether she can eat from *any* trees in the garden.

Eve corrects him with her unfallen personal logic: "Of course we may eat fruit from the trees in the garden . . . It's only the fruit from the tree in the middle of the garden that we are not allowed to eat" (3:2–3). She's basically saying, "I'm a child of a generous God. I live in a free world with only one rule. I get what I need by eating from every tree but the one that will kill me."

But the Serpent replies, "You won't die!" He pushes back on Eve's worldview. "That fruit is not deadly. You don't live in that kind of world." Then he moves to question one and challenges her identity, "God knows that your eyes will be opened as soon as you eat it, and you will be like God, knowing both good and evil" (3:5). In other words, "You are not the child of a kind and generous God. You're the subject of a stingy God who's holding out on you!"

Then Eve looked at the deadly fruit and saw that it was beautiful, delicious, and desirable. She wanted the wisdom it could give her. Once her personal logic is reframed, she is convinced. She eats. Adam eats. It makes complete sense in the moment. The original couple gain the fruit but lose themselves and lose their world.

This consequence is the inevitable tragedy of yielding to temptation. Each time you give in, you are losing ground, slipping away from the person God has created and redeemed you to be. Yielding to temptation, you're also tempted to believe you live in a lesser world and have a smaller identity than God has given you. And the crazy thing is, when you act on those lies, the lies come true.

A depressed mom feels trapped in a world without adventure. She escapes through online shopping. She opens a secret credit card account and tells herself she'll find a way to pay it off without her family knowing. With each click and new purchase, the balance keeps growing, as do the lies she fabricates to juggle finances and keep her secret hidden. She knows what she's doing isn't right, but she feels trapped in the cycle of debt and depression.

A young adult finds the thrill of online gaming exhilarating even as the losses add up. He fights the urge to bet, knows the risk, but the appeal of "one more bet" and the thought of winning compel him. Every time he opens a phone or mobile device, the opportunity is there. He can't resist.

A married manager senses an immediate attraction to someone at work. Office flirting leads to one-on-one lunches with every indication they could be something more. Loneliness at home intensifies the romantic fantasy and the idea of crossing lines previously prohibitive grows with each flirty text, sexy glance, or lingering touch.

A man finds himself on the road for work, alone in a hotel room, tired and exhausted. He tells himself he will no longer look at porn, but in the moment, he suspends all judgment and watches anyway. In the morning, he promises himself and God that he won't do it again, knowing he wants to give it up but rarely resisting the opportunity.

In each case, a world shrinks and a person gets more and more lost, but it doesn't have to spiral out of control this way. You can hang on to who you are. And it starts by clarifying your personal logic and basing it on God's truth. Remind yourself of who you are and the kind of world you live in. Then, when temptation arises, stop and realize that you can't get what you really want without God. That's when his promises can give you the power to cling to truth and to see through the enemy's lies.

THE FIGHT

Resisting temptation is not like flipping a switch. Temptations come into our lives both from within and from without. The Bible clearly teaches that you're caught in a spiritual battle. You have a spiritual adversary who wants to hold you down in destructive habits and patterns—to rob you of your identity and to make you lose sight of God's promises.

You don't have to look for the fight—at some point the fight will find you, and the enemy doesn't fight fair. You will get sucker punched and it will hurt. And you will feel like swinging back, but you have to know how to fight this spiritual battle. Paul writes, "For we are not fighting against flesh-and-blood enemies, but against evil rulers and authorities of the unseen world, against mighty powers in this dark world, and against evil spirits in the heavenly places" (Ephesians 6:12).

It's often easy for us to reduce the devil and the unseen world to the punch line from a joke, a scare tactic from horror movies, or a lyric from a song, like the Rolling Stones' "Sympathy for the Devil." The devil becomes a pop culture reference or something from a skit on *Saturday Night Live*. And in our age of science and technology, believing in the devil and a spiritual world can seem far-fetched and superstitious.

But if you take Jesus seriously, you have to take the unseen world seriously. In the Bible, Jesus often interacts with dark spiritual forces. He casts out demons and shows authority over them. He speaks of Satan and challenges us to be aware of our enemy's ongoing agenda.

Bottomline: the devil is a tempter. When Jesus was baptized, God spoke, heaven opened, and it was a huge public triumph. God said, "This is my dearly loved Son, who brings me great joy" (Matthew 3:17). He confirmed Jesus' identity openly and powerfully. Immediately afterward, this identity was tested. Jesus was led into the wilderness for forty days where he was tempted by the devil. Two of the three temptations begin with the phrase, "If you are the son of God," followed by a test. They are immediate challenges to Christ's identity and to who he claims to be. They are challenges to who God has just declared him to be in his baptism.

Jesus, however, did not fail the test. He did not let doubt compromise his identity. He clung to what he knew was true and with each temptation referenced Scripture to reinforce his decision to resist.

Sometimes God leads you into the wilderness and allows your identity to be tested. You have been told that God loves you, that he's in control, that he has a plan, but your life situation doesn't seem to match up with who God says you are. You ask, "Why am I going through this? Why did I get this diagnosis? Why did my car break down again? Why does it seem like everything is coming down around me? Why me?"

These are natural questions to ask in the wilderness. The wilderness is a test to move you forward in the journey of self-discovery and God discovery. The lessons you learn will prepare you for the blessings of the next season.

Another important principle we see in Jesus being led to the desert is that a testing often follows a triumph. Maybe you've taken a huge step in your spiritual life recently. You've forgiven a grudge you have held for years. You have started to trust God financially; you have started activating your faith. You have won major victories over temptation. Don't be surprised if things feel harder before they feel easier. When you push back the darkness, the darkness pushes back. You find yourself facing difficulties and don't understand. Yet, difficulty teaches humility, which empowers your future victory.

In the difficulty, in the wilderness, you learn to rely on God and stand firm. You learn life isn't all about you, and this opens your heart for God to use you more moving forward. So stand firm in the testing. The testing that follows the triumph prepares you for your purpose. Don't let the testing become a ground to give in to temptation. Remember your core identity, who God says you are.

DESIRE WITHIN

I once saw a sign that read, "Lead me not into temptation. Oh, who am I kidding, follow me—I know a shortcut!" Temptation comes not only from the devil and spiritual forces outside of you, but it also comes from within. James describes the nature of temptation this way: "Temptation comes from our own desires, which entice us and drag us away. These desires give birth to sinful actions. And when sin is allowed to grow, it gives birth to death" (James 1:14–15). Satan may be the ultimate cause of temptation and sin, but many temptations come from your own heart.

James uses powerful language to convey this. The phrase "drag us away" comes from hunting when an animal is lured into a trap. The animal is compelled by desire for the bait and then becomes trapped. Your desires also "entice" you, which is a fishing term. The bait is set and dropped into the water. The fish sees food and goes for the bite. The fish isn't thinking that this is the end or that this will lead to something else. The fish just sees the bait and thinks it looks good. The end result is being hooked and pulled out of the water. The fish is going for something to satisfy its desire, but it ultimately becomes lunch.

When you are tempted, when the trap or hook is baited by something that looks good, you are lured away by your own desires. This desire itself is not necessarily sin, but when the desire "gives birth" or "conceives" actions, sin comes into being. When you let it grow, it gives birth to death.

While God may test or prove his people in order to strengthen their faith, he never seeks to induce sin. James says that God, "never tempts anyone else" (James 1:13). God may test you to perfect your faith, but he doesn't tempt you to destroy your faith. He provides a way to bear up in the temptation or he shows you a way out.

WHAT LIES BENEATH

Victory in temptation is a hard code to crack. There is a lot involved beneath the surface of your life. You can pray, ask for help, and get insight from others, but you also need to look within at what is going on beneath the surface in problem areas.

Looking at our motives reminds me of when my daughter was a toddler. One day she decided it would be fun to pour Cheerios all over the floor. I asked her to stop and then picked them up. Later, she did it again. Lori said, "Emma, what are you doing? Why did you do that?" Completely innocent, our daughter said, "*I* didn't do it. My *hands* did it."

Doesn't she speak for all of us? You do something you shouldn't do and blame it on something else. My hands did it. It's because of your past or because you were with certain people. Your circumstances led you to do it. You want to blame everything and everybody before you accept responsibility, but responsibility is what leads to freedom. And sometimes the responsible thing is to take a look under the hood of your emotional life.

One of the most impactful books I've read is *Emotionally Healthy Spirituality* by Pete Scazzero. Pete had this moment when he realized that even though he'd been a Christian for twenty years and a pastor for ten, he was emotionally immature. He was still controlled by hurts from the past. He still argued and behaved in ways that modeled the dysfunction of his parents, and their parents, rather than the grace and wisdom of Jesus.

Accepting Christ does not magically make you emotionally mature and healthy. Jesus sets you free from the *penalty of your past*, but you may not be set free from the *pattern of your past*. You can be a Christian and know a lot about the Bible. You can be a follower of Jesus for decades and seem spiritually mature at church, and you can still be an emotional infant.

Maybe some of you come from a family where people claim to be spiritually advanced but are also really mean. They are filled with anger or sarcasm. They don't make any effort to engage or identify with others. They are horribly insensitive or distant. That is not spiritual maturity; it's emotional immaturity. These are individuals who have never learned to process the hurts under the hood, and you might be processing all of your emotions in the same dysfunctional way you learned from them.

Spiritually, I knew a lot about the Bible after college and graduate school, but I still had many areas where I needed to grow up emotionally, and I still do. I have to deal with what is going on under the hood so that my spiritual and emotional maturity come together. When you separate spiritual and emotional maturity, you end up with people who attend church every weekend, know their Bibles, but are rage-aholics, guilt-trippers, super-critical, unloving and uncaring at home. They've separated their spiritual life from their emotional maturity and health and that means that their emotions are running their life rather than God. They can't resist temptation because they can't control emotion.

In her book *Rising Strong*, Brené Brown coined a phrase called "chandelier-ing."[20] She got it from her husband who is a pediatrician. He says there are some injuries that hurt so bad, that even when you touch them gently, the person jumps so high they hit the chandelier. Brené goes on to say that in her experience as a social worker and shame-researcher, she's found that people's emotional pain can be the same way. Some emotional wounds are so painful that when another person barely touches on the issue, you hit the chandelier.

Maybe you felt abandoned by someone as a child or had an important promise broken. The wound is still there and when a small thing happens, like a person is late for lunch, you hit the chandelier. Or your spouse leaves the argument to cool off and this feels like abandonment, so you hit the chandelier. Maybe someone who was supposed to look out for you broke your trust instead. Now, whenever you feel threatened or you need to trust someone in a big way, you hit the chandelier. Maybe a friend or authority figure shamed you in a significant way. Now when a person teases you in a lighthearted way, you hit the chandelier. A boss or teacher or parental figure corrects you, and you hit the chandelier. The hurt is so deep that when anything gets close to it, when you feel like the experience is happening again, you start chandelier-ing.

These emotions are so powerful that you obey them without thinking. You may not even realize you are having an emotional reaction. One of the simplest and most powerful things you can do is to simply stop and acknowledge that you are indeed feeling something powerful. Your heart is trying to tell you something. It may not be right, but it wants to be heard. And then you can put a name to that emotion so you know what it is warning you about. Finding out what your triggers are emotionally can then help you step toward the freedom God offers over temptation.

Our feelings themselves are not sinful—it's how we respond in our thoughts and actions that usually leads to temptation. The important thing to see about emotions, even the ones you consider undesirable, is that they all have a purpose. Anger is what helps you to deal with threats. Sadness is how you process loss. Fear keeps you out of danger.

Disgust keeps unhealthy things out of your life. Guilt lets you know when you're violating an important value. Joy, love, and surprise are great feelings that make it wonderful to be a human. We all want more of them, and I believe ultimately we find all of those feelings fulfilled in a relationship with Jesus.

Acknowledging and naming the emotions going off in your life is hard work to decipher on your own. A counselor or spiritual mentor can be very important to help you process. I've benefited greatly from having others help me figure out what is going on under the hood. All of this is in an effort to help you overcome the destructive habits and patterns you struggle with. To help you live in the promise of victory over temptation, to help you master your emotions through God's power so that they don't master you.

DOWNLOAD SOME WISDOM

Sometimes when you go through trials or temptations, you have a hard time making sense of it. James says, "If any of you lacks wisdom, you should ask God, who gives generously to all without finding fault, and it will be given to you" (James 1:5, NIV). When you can't find your way out of a temptation, ask God for wisdom. Wisdom will be your guide though the troubles and temptations you face. It's the means through which you understand and live out God's will in your life. James is not just giving advice here; this is a command. You need God's wisdom to face your temptation. Nobody else can provide you with what God can provide.

When your trial overwhelms you and you are tempted to binge drink, or purge yourself, or go shopping with money you don't have, ask God for wisdom. When you just aren't making ends meet, even though you work hard and don't spend like crazy, ask God for wisdom. When you have to make a tough decision for your family, ask God for wisdom.

You may feel like the bad things in your life are winning. You keep eating the cupcake. It feels too late for you, like temptation has thrown you a knockout blow, but the real hit happened when Jesus died and rose again and delivered the knockout to the devil. Jesus won this fight and he's in your corner. He is the undisputed heavyweight champion of the universe, and your role is to stand firm in the fight he already won.

Stand firm in your forgiveness and in the hope of eternal life. Stand firm in the belief that God will help you face your temptation. Stand firm on the promise that he will show you a way out, that victory is possible. Stand firm and trust that with God all things are possible. Stand firm in faith when you want to stand down. You may still have to fight, but Jesus will never lose the fight and he will not lose you. Temptation is never easy, but God will always show you a way out so you can stand firm and hang on to who you really are.

And when you fail, God offers his remarkable grace.

CHAPTER 7

PLAN Z

Perhaps more than ever, our world often feels like a dangerous, precarious place. Economic ups and downs send us worrying about another downturn and its impact on our job, our home, and our retirement account. Terrorism continues to gnaw at our fears with more invasive strikes in heavily populated, often public places. Mass shootings in schools, malls, and offices leave us wary and on edge as we go about our daily routines. And these are just the big things—not to mention the more personal issues, like our health and relationships, we all face from time to time.

No wonder then that this next promise of God is among the most popular and best known: *I will give you a future and a hope.* This promise comes from the famous passage in Jeremiah: "'For I know the plans I have for you,' says the Lord. 'They are plans for good and not for disaster, to give you a future and a hope'" (29:11). This is what we all want out of life. We want things to get better. We want the future to be a place worth working toward. We need a sense that someone is guiding this crazy thing called life.

Like many others, I love this verse and frequently draw hope and confidence from it, but when taken in isolation, it can mess with your expectations. It seems to draw a straight line from where you are to where God wants you to be—or where you think God should want you to be. You think, *If God makes the plans, there will be no disasters. Just non-stop, incremental progress. Things will get better and better. Terrible things won't happen—or if they do, not as often.* But when things don't go as you hoped and expected, you start to lose confidence. Maybe God's not leading you where you thought you were going. Maybe he's not even in control. Maybe he doesn't care about your well-being.

But those feelings are just that—feelings—and not the truth.

No matter all evidence to the contrary, you can stand on his incredible promise: "I will give you a future and a hope." We've seen how this future and hope center on God's presence. We've looked at how God's work in Jesus and his power through the Holy Spirit empower our future. We are completely set free from condemnation and filled with the Spirit. This results in love, joy, peace, patience, goodness, gentleness, and self-control. We've considered his promise to bless and how this changes how we view the future. The old mixtape that traps us in our past is gone and a new mix-tape plays now. Temptation is an ongoing fight, but God promises us the victory through faith.

Keeping in step with God means letting his promises set the tempo for your life. God not only promises his presence, but he offers his purpose. He does not give you purpose instead of problems but alongside whatever problems may pop up. God has a perfect future in store for you, but that future begins in the imperfect now, in the present, no matter how poorly your plans may appear to be going. The real power of the promise of Jeremiah 29:11 is in understanding the historical context. Often we hang on to this promise in a vacuum, but grasping the original situation of those who received this promise resets expectations and fills our hearts with faith.

BROKEN DREAMS

The people who originally received this promise for a future and a hope were facing their own worst nightmare. Jeremiah was writing to some Israelites who'd just been dragged from their homes and taken as prisoners to a foreign land. All of their dreams, hopes, and desires had crashed to the ground as they landed in their worst-case scenario: *exile*.

Their country had been overthrown by the Babylonians, and they lost everything: homes, land, money, farms, fields, livestock, familiarity, language, culture, and hopes for their future and their kids' futures. All of it was gone, but what was most painful was the destruction of the temple. God's presence dwelt in the temple; it was a picture of God's special relationship with Israel. When the temple was destroyed, it appeared that God's presence had left them. The most special thing in their universe was raked to the ground. The psychological and physical devastation must have been massive.

When God spoke through Jeremiah, saying, "I know the plans I have for you, plans for good and not disaster," they would have looked around and seen nothing but destruction, pain, and difficulty. Plan A was over. Plan B was impossible. These were people with no plan left at all. They were living a nightmare and there was no waking up. This was plan Z.

To make matters worse, people claiming to be prophets of God gave them false messages of optimism. They declared that the captivity would not last long. God would lead them back home in eighteen months! Two years tops! The message landed on willing ears. These people didn't want to deal with the darkness. They wanted the sun to come out. They wanted this exile over, but the false prophets were singing out of key. The dream they were selling was a lie.

So God sent his true prophet, Jeremiah, to drop a truth bomb on his people: "Do not listen to their dreams, because they are telling you lies in my name. I have not sent them" (Jeremiah 29:8-9). This is a caution for us today. Not everyone who shares an encouraging word is called by God. Not every dream is one sent from God. Smart people believed these false dreams in the ancient world, and smart people believe false dreams today.

You pick up your personal dreams from a lot of places—culture, family, friends, movies, music, and entertainment. You may have lots of dreams—a fitness dream, a financial dream, a career dream, or a family dream. They may be powerful and beautiful. I hope they come true. Just don't pursue your dreams at the expense of God's ultimate purpose for your life because what he has for you is always better than anything you can dream up on your own.

MAKING GOOD TABLES

God says, "I know the plans I have for you," but how do you discover these plans? How do you claim this promise and find that greater dream and future? These questions can lead you to one of the most paralyzing questions of faith: "Why am I here? What is my calling? What's unique about what I have to offer?"

Calling sometimes seems so daunting and mysterious that you can miss the obvious. You may have hidden talents that God intends to use, but God's purpose is not so hidden, and his call is quite clear: you are called to know him and to serve him.

Os Guinness makes a helpful distinction between our primary calling, secondary calling, and special calling in his book *The Call*.[21] We already know God's macro dream for the world—that people will believe in Jesus and find their salvation and hope in him. So our primary calling is to believe in Jesus and surrender each day to him. Jesus said, "This is the only work God wants from you: Believe in the one he has sent" (John 6:29). You are called to faith in Christ and to trust him. Before you get caught up in what God has called you to *do*, remember God has first called you to *be*.

You're called to *someone* before you're called to *something* or *somewhere.*

We also have a clear secondary calling: to use our time, talent, and resources to serve God by serving others. This attitude grows out of responding to our primary calling. It's a mindset that realizes all you have is to bring honor and glory to God.

Historically, the church messed up a lot of our thinking with a troubling distinction. They viewed the "perfect life" as one dedicated to sacred jobs and vocations—things like being a priest, a nun, or a monk. The other category was the "permitted life" which was everything else—being a tradesman, working a craft, creating art, being a soldier, farmer, homemaker, salesperson, etc. Life was divided into the sacred (valuable things done in church), and the secular (less valuable things done in the world).[22] It implied that we can only serve God by working in a specifically religious context, but this is a distincition the Bible does not make. God is with us every day, not just Sundays. He'll meet you in every moment, not just those you spend at church. God cares about your work.

Your role as a teacher, salesperson, manager, CEO, parent, homemaker, artist, or craftsman is equally valid to my role as a church leader. Our main calling is the same—to believe in Jesus and to surrender to him. Our secondary calling is the same—to use our time, talent, and resources to serve him by serving others. Dorothy Sayers put it this way, "The Church's approach to an intelligent carpenter is usually confined to exhorting him not to be drunk and disorderly in his leisure hours, and to come to church on Sundays. What the Church should be telling him is this: that the very first demand that his religion makes upon him is that he should make good tables."[23]

God calls you to do everything for his glory. Be a faithful police officer for God's glory. Serve your family as a stay-at-home parent for God's glory. Wait tables to the best of your ability for God's glory. Testify through your life about God's mercy and his avaliablity to others. Give God glory by doing a good job. Make good tables.

This secondary calling, to use our gifts to serve God, is less defined and more entrepreneurial. It's about branching out and taking some risks. Take whatever you are good at—your business skills, your creative expression, your organizational ability, your passions—and put them to work. Take the opportunities presented to you. Solve the problems that bother you. Fill the obvious needs. Make a difference to someone or a group of someones.

You may even find a dream welling up in your heart. You don't have to wait and wonder if your dream is something you are specifically called to do by God. Just honor the purposes he has already revealed. You are called to know Christ and to share Christ with all you are and all you do. This call is your guiding purpose in life. If your inner dream lines up with his expressed purposes, that's a green light. Give it a try! Nothing you ever do for the Lord is useless. He may bless you in surprising ways. God often uses your faithful service to recover something valuable in yourself. As you give back to others in love, God restores and redeems some piece of who you really are.

GOD USES YOUR YOU-NESS

The third type of calling Os Guiness pointed out is a special calling. The special calling is a call to serve God's purpose for a specific time doing a specific task. God reveals his special calling in powerful and supernatural ways in the Bible. These examples are often what we think of when we want to know our own "calling" or "God's dream for us" because it comes with specific guidance from God. We see this most clearly in the prophets of the Old Testament. God called these individuals to speak to a particular issue in a particular way.

We are tempted to use language like: "I'm not sure if God is calling me to this job, or calling me to marry this person, or calling me to attend this church." Our egos really like the idea of a special calling, but Os Guinness points out that a special calling in the Bible is almost always the task of challenging others to wake up to their primary and secondary callings. When God gives a special calling, it is somehow connected to helping others embrace faith, to return to God, or to live for him with their lives. God's special calling simply challenges people to engage the first two callings.[24]

If you don't know what your specific calling is yet, that's okay. Many people in the Bible *never* received a specific calling! This doesn't make you less important because every believer already has a primary calling to follow Jesus and a secondary calling to use your gifts and talents to serve God by serving others right where you are. All of this should empower you to go after the things you love to do but to do them for God's glory.

You don't need to wait for God's voice or some dramatic event to discover why you are on this planet. God will use as much of your life as you surrender to him. There are times when you must wait on God, but often God is waiting on you. He is waiting to respond to faith. He is saying, "Give me something I can bless."

One way you can clarify your dream is to seek God through prayer. Pause on a regular basis and pray, "God, the company I'm building, the career path that I'm on, the relationship that I'm entering, is this the right path for me?" Just by praying about a situation, you've already taken an important step. You're inviting God to guide you.

Another important quality is surrender. Are you willing to take your dreams and goals and lay them down before God? Are you willing to let them go if God desires something else for you? If you're not willing to surrender a dream, then that dream holds a higher position in your life than God. It's good to follow your dreams, but it's essential to follow Jesus. Only he has plans to give you a future and a hope.

The difference between magnificence and mediocrity is often mold-ability. Are you willing to have your life—your time, your energy, your efforts, and output—shaped by God? Are you willing to let him mess with you? You may want to be the finished piece of art standing proud on God's table, but are you willing to be the clay?

Wise counsel is also important. God speaks to you through his Word and his Spirit. He speaks through other people and circumstances. Seek wise counsel. Get around smart, intelligent, spiritually mature people. Search out someone older and ask them for insight. Pursue wisdom. Look at your situation, at what God has been revealing to you through prayer and his Word, at the wise voices around you. It can help you reconsider how your dream can align with God's greater purpose.

NO TIME TO WAIT

Just because you have clarity about a dream or goal doesn't mean you have the timing. God says to those impatient exiles, "You will be in Babylon for seventy years. But then I will come and do for you all the good things I have promised, and I will bring you home again'" (Jeremiah 29:10). This may sound hopeful to us at first glance, but it must have been a crushing announcement at the time. While the false prophets and fortune tellers told them they would be home just around the corner, God says it will be seventy years!

This news meant many who received this message were never going back. They would live the rest of their lives in exile. They would never rebuild in Jerusalem, never see some of their old friends again, never see their homes again. The dream was awesome; the timing was awful.

You can jettison a lot of stress and anxiety by simply acknowledging that God, not you, controls both the dream and the timing. While you are waiting for the future and hope to take shape, God is forming and shaping you. Seventy years was a long time to wait, but God was protecting the Israelites. Back home in Jerusalem there was war, conflict, and difficulty. God kept the exiles safe in Babylon. He protected them in those years when they couldn't see what he was doing.

I often assume that because I have a dream, I can expect immediate fulfillment. When I have prayed it through and received wise counsel, and when my dream is in line with God's purposes and my passion, sometimes I charge ahead only to smash into the brick wall of reality. Rather than wait on God to open the right doors, I kick at the right door at the wrong time. It was God's dream, but my deadline.

You may have the dream, but God's deadline might be years from now. You may feel exiled because God isn't opening doors. Just because you can't see God moving in your circumstances doesn't mean he isn't moving. The Israelites couldn't see it, but God was working while they were waiting. The dream was right, but the timing was later.

You may feel like God isn't showing up right now. You may not be sure you can keep going. You may feel like your destiny has been derailed or the miracle has been missed, but it hasn't. You aren't alone, abandoned, forgotten, left behind, or picked over. You aren't disqualified and your story isn't finished. You don't have to know what's going to happen next when you trust your destiny to the God of yesterday, today, and tomorrow. You can step out and obey even in the uncertainty because God has got this, and he's got you.

WORK WHILE YOU WAIT

I like speed. Nothing moves fast enough for someone who values quickness and efficiency, like deplaning at the airport after arriving at the gate. We pull up, the fasten seatbelt sign dings, and everybody jumps up. You've got people bent under the overhead bins, halfway in the aisle, bags on their shoulder. We're all ready to get off that plane.

Then a time warp happens. Things sloooooow doooooown. People fumble with their stuff. They slowly pull themselves out of their seats. They take precious seconds to engage the handles on their wheel bags. It's all I can do to keep from rushing the people in front of me: "Help her with that bag! Move people! I need to get home!"

It's times like this that I forget about the process. Unloading a cabin full of people takes time. Most stuff in life rarely happens as fast as I imagine it will. This is where the exiles are at emotionally. They want this thing to be over quickly. They are ready to get off the plane and get on with their lives, but God has a process underway.

Jeremiah delivers God's orders, "Build homes, and *plan to stay*. Plant gardens, and eat the food they produce. Marry and have children. Then find spouses for them so that you may have many grandchildren. Multiply!" (Jeremiah 29:5–6)

A lot of times when you hear that God has a plan for you, you think about the future. You imagine entering into something better than the mess you are dealing with now. Jeremiah reminds us that even the exile—the thing they wanted out of—is a part of God's plan. They saw it as their problem; God used it as a process.

God commands these people to get busy while they wait. It's not the message they want, but it is the message they need. God may be saying to you, "Prepare to stay here a while." Even if the reasons are unclear, preparing to stay prepares you to learn. Focusing on the now moves you from magical thinking about tomorrow to empowerment today. It makes sure you don't become less while you are waiting on more.

God tells them straight up: "Do not dwindle away!" (29:6) The term "dwindle" means to "diminish gradually." This would have been a huge temptation with all the unknowns around them. When you are hurting and facing uncertainty, there's a temptation to pull back from others and fade away. You stop setting goals and seeking a better future. Depression and discouragement set in. You miss out on moments. Don't let the holding pattern hold you hostage. Move forward. Refuse to close up the blinds. Don't dwindle.

You've heard the phrase, use it or lose it? It's true in many areas of life. If you don't use the brains, time, skills, and gifts God's given you, they will dwindle. The opposite is also true: use it and gain it. The responsible get more reward. Those that risk and invest and try to multiply please God.

Those who hide, who bury their abilities, who are too afraid or lazy to try, who are just trying to hang on to what they have . . . they lose the little they are trying to protect. It's like a muscle—the more you use it, the stronger it becomes. The less you use it, the weaker it becomes. If you do nothing new, you become nothing new—you dwindle.

If you risk and commit, you multiply.

CONNECTION, NOT CLARITY

Sometimes we miss what's right in front of us because we're waiting for some "big sign" from God. Brennan Manning told a story about a brilliant ethicist who went to go work with Mother Theresa in Calcutta for three months. He was on a journey to decide how to live the rest of his life and wanted some clarity. On the first morning, he met Mother Teresa who asked, "And what can I do for you?"

He asked her to pray for him. "What do you want me to pray for?" she asked. He voiced the request that he had carried thousands of miles from the United States: "Pray that I have clarity."

"No, I will not do that," she said. "Clarity is the last thing you are clinging to and must let go of." He said that she always seemed to have the clarity he longed for and she laughed. She said, "I have never had clarity; what I have always had is trust. So I will pray that you trust God."[25]

Don't cling to clarity; cling to God.

What if God told you every detail of his plans—his huge, scary, wonderful plans that demand more of you than you ever imagined? Would that make it any easier to trust him? Would it make it any easier to take the first step? No, because trust *is* the first step. Connection creates trust when there is a lack of clarity, so seek connection over clarity.

Listen to how God's promise continues to unfold: "In

those days when you pray, I will listen. If you look for me wholeheartedly, you will find me. I will be found by you" (Jeremiah 29:12-14). That is a promise not of clarity, but of connection. He asks you to seek with your whole heart. To want to know him even more than you need to know the plan. To build your trust by leaning on his understanding rather than your own. To grow the faith you need for what comes next.

Eventually God does return the exiles home. The first wave of Israelites are sent back twenty years sooner than the seventy years. It was an 800-mile march. When they arrived, the land and culture were in disarray. It took a lot of hard work and courage to rebuild. More than all that, it took faith. They needed God's presence most of all. To take hold of God's purpose, they needed to trust his presence. They tapped in to the strength they developed while waiting on God's plan to unfold so that when the door opened, they were ready.

God is asking you to trust him with a next step. He's saying, "Let's go on a journey together, for I know the plans I have for you." Knowing the plan and going on the journey are two different things. The plan rarely comes with total clarity; it demands connection. You cannot enter his greater future without the faith it takes to get you there.

My dad exemplified this in more ways than one. Working in commercial refrigeration his whole life, he dreamed of working at a company that treated employees with integrity, acted morally, and did what they promised to do. One day he sensed God was leading him to start that business. He said, "Since I can't find that company, apparently I'm going to have to start my own."

He started in a friend's basement. The big challenge was money. He applied for small loans to acquire the basic gear needed to get the business going but kept getting rejected. Finally, my dad met with an older gentleman known for taking risks on people. He walked in, praying the whole time. He said, "Okay, God. Please give me the words and the right things to say."

When they met, the first words out of my dad's mouth were, "You look like my grandfather." As soon as he said it, he thought, "You dummy! You just messed this thing up. This guy will never loan you any money now." But those words changed the whole direction of their conversation.

The older man said, "Tell me about your grandfather." That began a rich conversation that had nothing to do with the business. The man talked about his own life, and his own grandfather and father. Within a short time he had tears in his eyes. Then he broke it off and said, "Well, Mr. Wilhite. You have your loan." My dad shook his hand and walked out. Everything that appeared to go wrong had worked out just right. That began a thirty-year journey, and my dad ran his business until he retired.

He sums it up like this: "I wasn't smart enough to do it myself, but God works in mysterious ways. God had a plan. God had a purpose." Dad had to keep getting up every day and doing the best he could do. He had to run the business the way he dreamed. It wasn't easy. There were good days and bad. In one economic downturn, he was reduced to putting almost everything he owned up for collateral, but through it all he trusted God. He honored his Creator, and God honored him. My dad was in the refrigeration business, but his calling was from God. He fulfilled his primary calling and trusted in Christ. He lived out his secondary calling by using his time, talent, and resources to serve God and serve others. He left this world a better place than he found it. His is a legacy of love and character.

You have a need for purpose. To know that despite all the problems, all the waiting, all the twists and turns, that life is heading some place good and better is on the way no matter how harsh things may seem in the present. To know that God is in control and really does care about you and wants what's best for you.

God promises the best is yet to come and will see to it himself. You don't need to plan the perfect life. You just need to trust your perfect Savior. He knows the plans, but you can know the Planner, and he's dreaming up more than you can even imagine.

CHAPTER 8

WEAVER OF DREAMS

Living means the unexpected happens—things you could never imagine suddenly transpire before your very eyes. That was my experience recently when I heard a sound like a shotgun blast coming from our garage. Had our hot water heater exploded? Were we having an earthquake? Had someone driven by and actually fired a gun into our home?

Before I tell you what actually happened, let me back up. When our daughter turned sixteen, we passed Lori's older car on to her and bought a newer one for Lori. There was no doubt that the new car would get the coveted spot in our garage, keeping it out of the blistering heat we often experience here in Las Vegas. Everyone was happy with the Wilhite transportation situation—at least for a few days.

Less than a week after we had purchased Lori's car, however, I was working from home when I heard that epic explosion. Running out to the garage, I saw black paint dripping on everything in sight—including our new car. Then I saw the remains of a shredded can of Rustoleum spray paint, matte black.

Apparently, it had overheated in the gazillion-degree desert heat of our garage and exploded. It blew the lid off a plastic storage bin and rained down all over Lori's car, and I knew it would be almost impossible to get off.

The timing was conspicuous to say the least. Why had this never happened over the previous fourteen years but waited until we pulled a new car into the garage? It took countless hours and grit-your-teeth tenacity to get the paint off that car. But through it all, I noticed something different—my usual attitude to such events.

Somehow studying God's promises had changed me. He never promised me that paint wouldn't explode on our new car. This crazy, unimaginable stuff just happens and I don't know why. I'm on a need-to-know basis with God, and apparently I don't need to know. My job is to clean up the mess and be grateful that no one was hurt. I'm called to work hard with what God has given me, helping and serving others, and that includes moving all the cans of spray paint from our garage into the laundry room—and warning you, of course.

FOR GOOD

I don't know your situation, but I believe God is with you in it no matter what you may be going through. He is there, even when you can't see him, can't hear him. When you are hurting and lost, struggling in the pain, you can cling to this beautiful promise of God: *I will work all things for good.* We find this promise in this powerful verse: "And we know that in all things God works for the good of those who love him, who have been called according to his purpose" (Romans 8:28, NIV).

This promise is both tremendous encouragement and nail-biting frustration. Life is filled with people who don't seem to be doing very well. It is filled with people who lack faith but are winning; and people who have faith who appear to be losing. If God works for the good, why is there so much pain—natural disasters, tornadoes, tsunamis, terrorist attacks, acts of violence, and abuse? This promise is loaded with both mystery and comfort.

The challenge with a promise like this is to not project my doubt over someone else's suffering. Over the years, I've walked with hundreds of people going through the most unbelievable losses. It's tempting to look from the outside and question why God allows certain things to happen in their lives, but often those in the middle of those challenges don't share that same doubt. They experience deep grief, but also the peace, "which surpasses all understanding" (Philippians 4:7, ESV). God deepens their faith through the difficulty. They wouldn't wish their story on anyone, but they also wouldn't want their story to fuel someone else's doubt. Their faith has grown in the hardships. Personal questions, doubts, and struggles remain, but so does faith. So I choose to take courage from the strength the promise provides.

It's possible to be overexposed to this promise. We can

be vaccinated against its power. Familiarity reduces its impact. As I've reflected on it and reconsidered its depths, this promise immediately raises my spirits. The weight of life lifts from my shoulders. If I really believe it, then I have nothing to worry about. Nothing. Whatever comes tomorrow is covered by the unseen hand of God. Even if it is terrible, he will work it for good. He is always in my corner. This truth is one of the most beautiful promises in all of the Bible. Don't miss out on what it can do in your life just because it is familiar.

In no way is this promising that all things that happen to you are inherently good. Just before this verse Paul says that you will be glorified with Christ if you suffer with him, that your current pain can't compare to your future glory, that creation is subject to futility, that you groan as you wait for redemption, and that you are saved "in hope." You can't always see hope, otherwise it wouldn't be considered hope, yet it is precisely in this struggle and hurt that you realize God is working.

When Paul says God is working for the good "in all things," there is no qualification. All things includes *everything*. God steers and maneuvers *all* things to his end—the good, bad, righteous, and unrighteous. Whether he allows it or causes it, his hand is behind it. The only qualification of the promise is "those that love God." This is not a universal promise but a specific one intended only for believers.

We call this God's providence, which isn't a word we throw around a lot. The term literally means "to see beforehand." God sees all, which is his foreknowledge, but more than this foreknowledge, providence implies that he sustains all, as well. When God created the heavens and earth in Genesis, the term for "created" includes continued maintenance. God did not simply create and then let things run on their own. He sustains the world, and he sustains your life.

Providence gets to God's involvement in sustaining and guiding all of creation, both the realm of nature and people. It includes the tough things he permits and the good things he accomplishes, and it is filled with divine mystery. How God orchestrates events and works his will through free human beings is a puzzle that the greatest thinkers cannot solve.

Still, as God reveals himself in the Bible, you see his control everywhere. Jesus said that not even a sparrow falls to the ground outside of God's knowledge. The hairs on your head are numbered (see Matthew 10:–30). God works everything to go "according to his plan" (see Ephesians 1:11). Even "The king's heart is like a stream of water directed by the LORD; he guides it wherever he pleases" (Proverbs 21:1). The Psalmist describes each day of his life as being inscribed in God's book, "Every moment was laid out before a single day had passed" (Psalm 139:16).

Earlier generations were more familiar with providence. They talked of "the hand of Providence" and saw God moving and working behind the scientific framework of cause and effect. They wrote of God's ultimate, or first, cause. So much emphasis today is put on secondary cause and effect and chance. Everything gets reduced to what you can see and investigate, but chance is just a word, a mathematical possibility. It doesn't actually do anything, and the Bible doesn't leave room for random chance as it relates to the events of your life. God is above it and beyond it and working within it. This doesn't mean that there aren't real mysteries and "whys" as it relates to terrible things that happen, but it does give hope that God can actually do something about them.

THE PIT IS THE PATHWAY

Perhaps the greatest person in the Bible to show how God works all things for good is Joseph. Only seventeen when we meet him in the book of Genesis, Joseph was tasked with tending his family's flocks with his brothers, but there wasn't a lot of brotherly love for Little Joe. He probably didn't help matters by bringing his father a bad report about his brothers—nobody likes a tattletale. To make matters worse, his father, Jacob, loved Joseph more than his brothers and gave his favorite son a bright, beautiful robe. Joseph reveled in it, but his brothers seethed.

The tension mounted after Joseph received a dream. It was unlike anything he'd ever experienced. He and his brothers are binding sheaves of grain when suddenly his brothers' sheaves gather around his and bow down. Later, he has a second dream where the sun, moon, and eleven stars, like his eleven brothers, bow down to him.

In the ancient world, dreams were big business. There were dream interpreters who would catalog the meaning of dreams and study them like a science. It proved very profitable. Dreams also play a prominent role in the Bible as a way God communicates his revelation to people. Sixteen different dreams are recorded in the Old Testament where God reveals his will to people.

Joseph told his brothers about the dream and they understood the meaning immediately—their little brother thought he would rule over them one day. This honesty added more tension to already strained family relationships. Plenty of drama filled Joseph's life before he woke from the dream, and even more after he shared the dream.

One day, when the brothers are grazing their father's flocks, Jacob sends Joseph out to check on them. They see him coming from a distance because he wears the coat of many colors his father gave him. "Here comes that dreamer!" they say to each other (Genesis 37:19). In the original language, there is sarcasm: "Here comes the dream master, the guy who is going to rule over us. Yeah, right!" The brothers ambush him and throw him into a nearby well, declaring, "We'll see what becomes of his dreams" (37:20). Reality TV has nothing on this family!

Joseph found himself in a pit up to his knees in mud. The stone was probably replaced on the mouth, and it was pitch black. He can't see or hear anything. This is not the way it was supposed to go! His brothers are not bowing down; they are beating him down. What would have been unthinkable only hours before is now a reality for Joseph.

Have you ever found yourself in a similar pit? An event or tragedy occurs, you find yourself knee deep in betrayal or misfortune, and you wonder where God is. You get locked up in a painful, dark place where you can't see or understand what's happening. When God says that he'll work all things for good, does this include the pits of life? Yes, absolutely—in fact, the pits are his specialty.

No matter what you are facing, God is still in control. You may feel like hope is lost, but wherever God is, there is hope. The presence of pain in your life does not mean the absence of God. He is working in the light while you are waiting in the dark. Just because it looks like a dead end, doesn't mean it is a dead end. God turns dead ends into detours to prepare you for your destiny.

The pit is often the pathway to God's plan. He is with you on the mountaintop when life is going according to plan. He is with you in the pit when the plan disintegrates before your eyes. The pit is essential in preparing Joseph for the good that God planned for him.

DIVINE DETOURS

Joseph's troubles were just beginning. After throwing him violently into the pit, his brothers sit down for lunch. A group of merchants pass by and the brothers get the idea to sell Joseph off and make a little cash. They sell him into slavery for twenty shekels of silver, the equivalent of two years wages.

If you grew up with brothers, then you know what happens when you do something wrong. For instance, you are playing catch in the living room when suddenly one brother misses the ball. It hits Mom's special china, which falls off the desk and smashes on the floor. What do you do now?

You find an alibi. That's exactly what Joseph's brothers did. They took Joseph's coat of many colors and smeared goat blood all over it. They carried it back to their father and said, "Isn't this Joseph's coat? A ferocious animal must have ripped him to pieces." Jacob is devastated at the loss of his favorite son, and the weight of this massive lie weighs on the brothers.

Meanwhile, Joseph has a one-way ticket to Egypt. He is purchased by a man named Potiphar. This surely looked like the end of Joseph. His entire future, his dream, is a sham. He's gone from favored son to slave, but then the unexpected happens again. As the months go by, Potiphar promotes Joseph all the way to head of his entire estate. Joe becomes CEO of Potiphar, Inc. God is still working for his good even in bad circumstances.

Amazingly, there is no indication that Joseph spends any time blaming his brothers or the traders, though he had every right. What happened to him is horribly evil and devastating, yet he believes that God still works in his life. Rather than play the blame game, he refuses to be a victim. He is sold as a slave, but he does not live like a slave. He does not let others' sin put a label on him. Rather than waste his life pointing fingers at those who hurt him, he focuses his life on moving forward.

When bad things happen, we usually look for someone to blame. It's natural. You blame the refs when your team plays badly. You blame your boss, the tasks, the customers, or other employees when your work goes poorly. You blame your spouse, your ex, or your kids when those relationships go south. You blame the government or corporations when your finances implode.

Yet, Joseph's life reminds us of a key principle: You never *blame* your way to a *better* life. Blaming feels good, but it doesn't do much good. It's like a burp. It feels good to get it out, but it stinks and tends to push other people away. When you constantly blame others, you shift the responsibility for your life onto someone else.

Few things are more inscrutable than suffering and pain. While you may never understand why you go through things, you can position yourself to make the most of the life you have. At some point, you have to move past questions that can't be answered this side of heaven. If you trust God's providential hand working for your good, then you move past blaming others and move toward responsibility. You begin to learn and grow. You shift from "Why me?" to "What am I supposed to learn here?" So no matter how unfair your situation feels, believe God is still working. Refuse to be trapped by the blame game because nobody wins.

BREAK YOU TO REMAKE YOU

Recently, when I should have gone to bed, I kept channel surfing and came across a Twisted Sister documentary. Now before you judge me, you must understand that this band headlined the first concert I ever attended. While I can't recommend you watch the documentary—most of it was just wrong—the opening scene was nevertheless powerful. It showed the band playing in Europe at a televised concert that led to their breakthrough record deal.

Then everything stops and the screen goes to black until these words appear: 3,267 shows earlier. The documentary then goes back to the beginning. It took Twisted Sister more than ten years of touring and 3,267 shows before they were ever signed! And you thought they just got lucky. You might wonder why they aren't better! There is always a build up to the breakthrough, even for Twisted Sister.

We admire people's breakthroughs in work, art, or life, but we rarely consider the buildup that precedes the breakthrough. Spiritually, you come to your breakthrough only after your preparation. Often, God breaks you down to build you back up. Charles Spurgeon, the great pastor of the 19th century, asks: "Is it not a curious thing that, whenever God means to make a man great, he always breaks him in pieces first?"[26] Sometimes God breaks you to remake you. He breaks you of your self-reliance, pride, and stubbornness. He brings you into submission so you can be used more fully.

If things weren't hard enough already, Joseph is about to be broken at another level. When his life finally settles into a new routine as head of his master's household, Joseph is cornered by Potiphar's wife with a none-to-subtle, "Come to bed with me!" She continues to make passes and Joseph continues to refuse. At one point, she comes to him when nobody is around and throws herself on him. Joseph runs, but as he flees, she hangs on to his cloak.

Potiphar's wife clutches the cloak as her lustful passion turns to rage. She cries loudly and the attendants run in. She accuses Joseph of rape. When Potiphar hears, he is enraged and naturally throws Joseph in prison. From one detour to the next, from one horrible situation to another. Joseph calls the prison he was put into a "pit," the same word used to describe the cistern that he was thrown into by his brothers. The pit has become an inescapable place in his life.

But through this, Joseph had passed another test. They took his cloak, but they didn't take his character. People can take a lot of things from you. They can take your house, car, or jacket, but no one can take your character. You can give it away and surrender it, but no one can take it from you. God used Joseph powerfully because he proved faithful.

Genesis chapter 40 begins with a small but loaded phrase, "Some time later" (40:1). We are not told how much time passed since Joseph is unjustly thrown into the pit again. The only thing that we know is that time is passing. Minutes, hours, days, and years are wearing on Joseph. The young man we met as a teenager has reached his twenties. The face once admired by Potiphar's wife is now covered by a thick beard. Joseph's own words imply that this is a miserable hole. Imagine a cramped space, stuffy and far from the sunlight. Smells of stench fill the air as dust and filth cover everything with no regard for sanitation.

In this awful place, "They hurt his feet with fetters and placed his neck in an iron collar until God's time finally came!" (Psalm 105:18–19, TLB). The iron on his feet and neck weighs him down and chafes his skin. Years crawl past, "How God tested his patience!" (Psalm 105:19).

It can boggle your mind. Why wouldn't God just send him out into the world to make a difference? Why wouldn't he use Joseph as a young, handsome person full of strength? What is God doing?

Only in the rearview mirror do you get perspective on what God is doing in the present. In retrospect, you see that he's sharpening Joseph's character. He's teaching Joseph to serve out of vulnerability and brokenness. He's honing Joseph's leadership skills. Joseph could not free himself from the prison, but he could free himself *within* the prison. He is not free to leave, but he is free to serve. Free to be a person of character. Free to hope. Free to expect great things from God even though he's stuck in an unfair and impossible situation. He knew he was loved by a just God for whom nothing is impossible. Joseph is in a cage, but the cage never gets into Joseph.

The warden eventually puts Joseph in charge of everything. The text says that he, "had no more worries, because Joseph took care of everything. The Lord was with him and caused everything he did to succeed" (Genesis 39:23). God is with him in spite of all the crazy twists and turns his life is taking, and Joseph is learning how to administrate in many situations. God is building him up for his breakthrough.

You can gloss over this preparation and forget that the buildup is brutal. Joseph had to overcome bitterness and hate in his heart. He had to refuse to play the blame game. He would have had every reason, and excuse, to underachieve, emotionally check out, self-sabotage, or give up. He could walk around blaming Potiphar or the system that placed him there. He could rage against all kinds of personal injustices, but you don't see Joseph doing it. You see him build on what he had. He took what was in front of him and said, "Okay God, let's do it. Let me follow you in faith today." He focuses on what he can do to build up his situation right where he finds himself.

PREP SCHOOL

I know firsthand that real preparation is tough. After coming to faith at seventeen following a four-year drug addiction, I felt like my life was both restored and at a dead end. I tried to play in a rock band for a brief period but knew ultimately that wasn't in the cards for me because I felt compelled to serve God differently. Yet, high school had been rough. At my graduation, one of the faculty walked by and said sternly and without a smile, "I never thought I'd see you here."

I finally got the nerve up to go to college. My first English essay came back to me full of red ink. It had no paragraphs and looked like a disaster. My professor, Dr. Carol Snyder, leaned down, handed my paper to me and asked, "What happened to you?" Yeah, it was that bad.

I felt like college was impossible. Other people were having fun; I was hunkered down in the library making up for lost time. I taught myself how to type and how to write. I actually read high school English and math books to get up-to-speed with college. The first two years were hard. My teachers saw my effort and were very patient with me. What I didn't realize is that this was preparation. God was teaching me to grow up, to take responsibility, and to work hard. He was teaching me discipline. What I thought was a dead end actually taught me skills I use every day. I started at the bottom of my class and graduated at the top, which just means there is hope for everyone.

I'm not proud of the things I did while lost in an addiction. It's part of my story. It just isn't the end of the story. The lessons learned in the brokenness prepared me to help other broken people today. God worked even in my rebellion. He takes rebels, breaks rebels, remakes rebels, and releases them to be rebels with a cause.

Maybe you're praying for a breakthrough at work, in your finances, marriage, or career. Until God builds you up in preparation, you aren't ready for the breakthrough. The breakthrough will break you. To prepare, you must let God shape and form you. It's hard in the buildup, but Joseph's life screams a key value—the battle of preparation is largely won in not giving up.

Don't give up when your family or friends betray you, when loved ones abandon you, when life flips upside down, or when the plan goes from clear to crazy.

Don't give up when people kick you while you are down, when you can't *see* a way out, can't see a way up, can't see hope, can't see God.

Don't give up when you don't *feel* strong enough, talented enough or qualified, when circumstances look insurmountable, difficulties seem overwhelming, and opportunities are denied because of your background, mistakes, gender, race, or faith.

Don't give up when others quit, blame, move ahead of you, get promoted over you, or seem so much happier on social media. (They're not!)

Don't give up when it hurts, when you're tired, when it's hard, when you fail, when it's impossible, inevitable, unlikely, or unpopular.

Don't give up because at just the right time, you will receive a harvest of blessing: "So let's not get tired of doing what is good. At just the right time we will reap a harvest of blessing if we *don't give up*" (Galatians 6:9, emphasis added).

You don't get to determine the right timing; only God does that. In Joseph's life, he must have thought the right time was much sooner than God. It is hard to keep this kind of hope alive. It takes something out of you to keep believing that God will move. It takes energy to believe your best days are ahead when all you see are difficulties. It's challenging to believe when every time you try to move forward, something gets in the way.

This struggle explains why people just fade away and quit. They stop hoping and start settling. But Galatians says it will happen—when?—*at just the right time*! Don't break faith before you breakthrough. Every day you are getting closer. You will receive a harvest of *blessing* if you don't quit. How tragic would it be if you quit right before the breakthrough? How heartbreaking to go through the waiting and the preparation but to never experience the breakthrough? Don't stop believing that God is working for your good.

Hang in, hang on, and don't ever quit!

THE BREAKTHROUGH

Joseph didn't quit and neither does God. A dream got Joseph into trouble originally, and it was a dream that God used to lead Joseph to his breakthrough. This time it is Pharaoh's dreams that bring Joseph to his breakthrough. Pharaoh, the leader of Egypt, had two dreams that contained elements of the fantastic: seven lean cows eat up seven fat cows, and seven heads of grain from a single stalk are consumed by seven lean heads of grain.

When he wakes, Pharaoh is disturbed and does something unusual. He calls for the professionals—magicians and wise men—to interpret his dream, but no one can. Pharaoh's cupbearer then remembers Joseph interpreting his dream when he'd fallen out of favor and landed in prison. He mentions to Pharaoh that Joseph is skilled in dream interpretations. Looking for an answer to his dream riddle, Pharaoh calls for Joseph. For the occasion, the rags of the pit are taken off, Joseph is cleaned, and then he is presented to the supreme leader.

Pharaoh tells him the dreams and says, "I have heard it said of you that when you hear a dream you can interpret it" (Genesis 41:15, NIV). Here is Joseph's moment. He's before the most powerful man in the world. This is the time to talk about how gifted he is, to claim he is the man. This is like the ultimate job interview, and you put your best foot forward. "Pharaoh," he might have said, "I have extensive knowledge in dream interpretation. I could really help you on an ongoing basis, and I am currently available. By the way, the whole prison thing is a set up. I didn't do it. So if you'd like, I can interpret your dreams both now and in the future."

Instead Joseph answered Pharaoh, "I cannot do it. . ." Here is Joseph, in the moment of his life, and he says he cannot do it. This man is a different man from the one we met sharing with his family about how they will all bow down to him. He is now broken and remade. He is changed by the difficulties of prison life. God put him through so much to prepare him for so much more. He answers, "I cannot do it . . . *but God will give Pharaoh the answer he desires*" (Genesis 41:16, NIV, emphasis added).

The framework for those God breaks and remakes is this: *I cannot, but God can*. Joseph's confidence, power, and strength lie completely in God. His dependence on him is undeniable.

Joseph interprets the dreams. The seven fat cows represent seven years of abundance. The seven skinny cows are seven years of famine that follow. The famine will be so intense that the abundance won't be remembered. Then he presents an idea: tax the people for grain in the seven years of abundance and store it, then in the seven years of famine charge them for the grain they gave you. This allows the people to survive, and it makes Pharaoh a ton of money. Pharaoh must have thought, "Yes! They pay me for the grain that they gave me in the first place. I like this guy."

Then Pharaoh asks: "Can we find anyone like this man, one in whom is the spirit of God?" (Genesis 41:37,NIV). Notice he doesn't point to Joseph's business sense, talent, or ability but to God's Spirit in him. That's what marks him.

Pharaoh looks out and sees a person of integrity and character, seemingly forgetting that he just came from prison! Here is a man led by the Spirit of God.

Pharaoh does the remarkable, the unbelievable. He puts him in charge of his entire court. Everyone will take orders from him, except Pharaoh himself. Joseph is made second in command of Egypt. This is the third house that Joseph is in in charge of: Potiphar's, Jailhouse, and now Pharaoh's house. Joseph is given Pharaoh's signet ring so that he can act on his behalf and is adorned with the robes of management and the ride of royalty. He's given a chariot, the limousine of the day, and men went before him clearing the way, like an ancient version of what the Secret Service provides for elected officials.

Joseph rises from nothing to everything after being in two pits for thirteen years. He is given a new name, Zaphenath-Paneah, and a wife from a powerful Egyptian family. Only God can do something so miraculous in the life of Joseph, and only after the breakthrough can he make any sense of the years of breakdown.

ALL THINGS FOR GOOD

By the time the seven years of plenty are over, it's been twenty years since Joseph had seen the brothers who betrayed him. Famine strikes their land. Jacob, Joseph's father, sends his sons to Egypt to buy grain. The times are desperate, and it is Joseph who oversees the distribution of grain to the people. The Bible records this amazing scene: "So when Joseph's brothers arrived, they bowed down to him with their faces to the ground" (Genesis 42:6, NIV).

Twenty years before the brothers hated Joseph for his dream. Now they unknowingly bring it to life. They consider it a blessing to be in the presence of this powerful Egyptian who can give them life by giving them food. The entire world is being blessed through one person who has stayed faithful to God. Joseph's dream was not about people bowing to him, it was ultimately about helping others and bringing God glory.

Joseph recognizes his brothers, but they don't recognize him. Dressed in the garb of Egyptian management, he speaks with an interpreter. Over the next few months he hides his identity and tests their character, family loyalty, and honesty.

At one point they return for food. He calls them close and reveals he is their brother. He says, "and now, do not be distressed and do not be angry with yourselves for selling me here, because it was to save lives that God sent me ahead of you" (Genesis 45:5, NIV). The contrast between *you sold me,* but *God sent me* rings of providence. Even the most vicious and violent acts that humans do can be redeemed by God.

All the anguish of this story—a father who lost a son and thinks he is dead for two decades; a family eaten away by secrets and guilt; a future ripped away due to petty selfishness and immaturity; the dehumanization of slavery; the inability to speak up for oneself when falsely accused; the despair of prison—all of it and more is ultimately overseen by God. *God sent me*. God sends you through the fire to get you to the fulfillment.

After all he's been through, Joseph sees God's purpose in it as the great weaver of dreams. He says, "You intended to harm me, but God intended it all for good. He brought me to this position so I could save the lives of many people" (Genesis 50:20). That word *intended* literally means to "weave," like you would weave a basket or a garment.

His father wove together a coat and some favoritism, which did Joseph unintended evil. His brothers wove together a plan to do evil, but God took those very actions and wove together a much bigger plan for good—a plan to save the lives of many people. You are included in this statement. Joseph saved this Hebrew family that would eventually produce Jesus, the savior of all people. That's the *biggest* of the big pictures.

God weaves the evil done *to us* into good done for us, by us, and with us.

He can weave your divorce into healing for someone else going through a relational disaster. He can weave your bankruptcy into financial counseling for others. He can weave your loneliness into compassion and engagement with others who are forgotten. He can weave your doubts into answers for others whose faith is weak. He can weave your tragedies, your dark days, your detours into healing for your own heart and the saving of many others. Your story may be the light that lets someone else out of their darkness.

So take courage. Your story is still being written. The last chapter has not been penned. It's not too late. Trust the God who "works all things for good for those who love him and have been called according to his purpose." No matter how deep and dark your pit, God will lift you out.

CONCLUSION

ON WINGS LIKE EAGLES

God's promises release you to really fly. You don't have to flap around in the cage of your past or the cage of captivity, but instead you can soar into the glorious future God has for you. Isaiah writes, "But those who trust in the Lord will find new strength. They will soar high on wings like eagles. They will run and not grow weary. They will walk and not faint" (Isaiah 40:31). The term "trust" here could be translated as "wait" or "hope." Those who eagerly *hope* in God, and by implication his promises, will soar on wings like eagles.

Soaring isn't easy—in fact, only a few birds actually soar. Many flap and glide, but soaring involves having the wingspan to be lifted by invisible streams of air. Eagles can fly at tremendous speeds without any effort, simply by riding along on the wind currents. Most of the time, though, I fear we don't soar as much as we flap.

And the way we flap reminds me of the birds in a ridiculous video game called Flappy Bird. Playing the game, you flap and flap to keep your bird at the right height to make it between all these tubes. It sounds easy enough, but inevitably you hit a tube and that's it. You're dead. Game over. No extra lives or chances. No difficulty settings. No prizes or levels. Just endless, merciless crashing and dying as you try to get a high score that ultimately is, well, meaningless.

Here's the thing about Flappy Bird: *everything feels like it's against you*. The controls are against you. The rules are against you. The tubes are constantly shifting and no matter what your high score is, there's always a chance you'll die without getting a single point the next time you play. In other words, playing Flappy Bird feels like life some days.

Sometimes all you do is run in place and flap around. You want to fly from point A to point B—chase some dreams, improve your life, find some happiness, grow spiritually—but things come at you and then—bam!—everything you flapped for comes to a disappointing end. The world seems against you. Your boss seems against you. Your own body may feel against you.

But God is for you. You are not Flappy Bird—you are a one-of-a-kind masterpiece soaring like an eagle! And the wind beneath your wings is fanned by God's promises. They are love notes from your Heavenly Father constantly whispering, "I am *for* you."

His promises give you the courage to leave your cage of fear and bask in the joy of his freedom. His presence is your promise. He has secured your salvation through the golden chain of events that he has planned for you from the foundations of the world. He sends his Spirit to guide you and to empower you. He is planning a greater future, and he will work all things for your good. He will do it all and much, much more, but there is one thing he cannot do. He cannot believe for you. He is trustworthy, but you must be trusting. He is faithful and true, but you must have faith in him.

My hope is that you begin to take God at his Word and appropriate these promises through faith. It does not take much—even just a little mustard-seed of faith in God can do big things. Tiny acts of trust can add up to profound life change. God has your new name waiting for you, and as you endure, you grow into that name. You grow into the life you are made for.

God decided long ago that heaven would not be complete without you. He wants to be with you in all you do, to fill your life, and to use you to accomplish amazing things. The cage door is open. The sky is calling. It's time for you to soar!

ACKNOWLEDGEMENTS

I'm so thankful for the many people who have helped with this book and have inspired me to learn more of God's promises and embrace them. To Lori, thank you for being my best friend and partner. I love doing this journey of life with you and I cherish you. Your faith, love, strength, and courage continue to amaze me. Thanks for being my date for life and constant encourager. You are beautiful inside and out.

To Emma and Ethan, I wrote this book with you in mind. I wanted to capture what has been so important in my own faith journey and to pass it on to you. I started writing these words for my own benefit, but soon I was writing with you in my heart. These promises can support you and guide you throughout your lives, and it is my prayer that they will in every way.

A special shout out to Justin Jackson for your insight and help with this project in its early stages. Thanks for serving alongside me faithfully for almost fifteen years. You have marked many lives for God and good, including mine. And to Dudley Delffs for your excellence in editing and lifting this book to a much better place. It is always a joy to work with you. A huge thanks to Mike Foster for all the listening as I talked through these concepts and for helping me zero in on the message. Your friendship is one of the greatest gifts God has given me.

As I was completing this manuscript, my pastor Roy Wheeler, passed on from this life after over fifty years of faithful ministry. He was the first to believe I could be a pastor, and the one who gave me so many opportunities to grow and serve. Thank you, Roy, for your love for all people and for how you lived your faith. I stand on your shoulders.

ABOUT THE AUTHOR

Jud Wilhite is an author, speaker, and senior pastor of Central Church, a church founded in Las Vegas with over twelve locations nationally and internationally. Central is recognized as one of the largest and fastest growing churches in America. He is a bestselling author of several books, including *The God of Yes*, *Pursued*, and a study Bible for new believers, *The Uncensored Truth Bible for New Beginnings*. His teaching segments are heard nationally on K-LOVE radio. He and his wife, Lori, have two kids and live in the Las Vegas area.

NOTES

ONE. PRESENCE IS THE PROMISE

1. Gary Richmond, *A View from the Zoo*, reprint ed. 2015 (Gary Richmond Ministries, 1987), Kindle book, location 491-492.
2. George MacDonald, *Unspoken Sermons, Series I, II, and III* (Jersey City, NJ: Start Publishing LLC, 2012), Kindle book, location 2959.
3. John Piper, "Fear Not, I Am with You, I Am Your God" (June 20, 1993) http://www.desiringgod.org/messages/fear-not-i-am-with-you-i-am-your-god.
4. CNN "Star Survey Reaches 70 Sextillion" (July 23, 2003) http://www.cnn.com/2003/TECH/space/07/22/stars.survey/. See also http://www.universetoday.com/guide-to-space/stars/how-many-stars/ and http://www.esa.int/esaSC/SEM75BS1VED_extreme_0.html.
5. Rick McDaniel, "Faith Over Fear" (Nov. 5, 2014) http://www.christianpost.com/news/faith-over-fear-the-bibles-1-statement-is-dont-be-afraid-129050/.

TWO. LITTLE BLUE BOXES AND STAIRWAYS TO HEAVEN

6. John Murray, as quoted in John Stott, *The Message of Romans:*

Good News for the World (Downers Grove, IL: InterVarsity Press, 2001), 248–249.

7. John Stott, *The Cross of Christ*, (Downers Grove, IL: InterVarsity Press, 1986), 159-160.
8. Thomas Cahill, *The Desire for the Everlasting Hills* (New York: Nan A. Talese Publishing, 1999), 285–286.

THREE. A BREATH OF FRESH AIR

9. R. C. Sproul, *Who Is the Holy Spirit?* (Orlando, FL: Reformation Trust, 2012), 31.
10. Raniero Cantelemassa, *Come, Creator Spirit* (Collegeville, MN: Liturgical Press, 2003), 9.
11. Ibid., 27.
13. J. P. Louw and E. A. Nida, *Greek-English Lexicon of the New Testament,* 2nd ed. (New York: United Bible Societies, 1996), 641.
14. Bibles for America, "Three Greek Words for Life in the New Testament and How They Apply to Us" (March 9, 2014) http://biblesforamerica.org/greek-words-for-life/.
15. C. S. Lewis, *Mere Christianity* (New York: HarperCollins, 2009), 49.

FOUR. BOOMERANG YOUR BLESSINGS

15. Wayne Grudem, *Systematic Theology* (Grand Rapids, MI: Zondervan, 2004), 176.
16. Deborah Tannen, in Jessica Bennett, "They Feel 'Bless-

ed'" (New York Times, May 2, 2014). https://www.nytimes.com/2014/05/04/fashion/blessed-becomes-popular-word-hashtag-social-media.html?_r=0.

17. K. H. Richards, K. H., "Bless/Blessing" in D. N. Freedman, Ed., *The Anchor Yale Bible Dictionary* (New York: Doubleday, 1992), 754.

FIVE. A NEW MIXTAPE

18. Hilary Hanson, "Tyrannosaurus Rex Joseph Gold, Formerly Tyler, Changed Name Because It's 'Cooler'" (*Huffington Post*, May, 8, 2012) http://www.huffingtonpost.com/2012/05/08/tyrannosaurus-rex-joseph-gold-tyler-name-change_n_1500519.html.
19. Plato, *The Works of Plato, Vols. I & II,* trans. by Benjamin Jowett (New York: Cosimo Books, 2010), 108.

SIX. THE FORBIDDEN RED VELVET CUPCAKE

20. Brené Brown, *Rising Strong: How the Ability to Reset Transforms the Way We Live, Love, Parent, and Lead* (New York: Random House, 2015), 61-62.

SEVEN. PLAN Z

21. Os Guinness, *The Call: Finding and Fulfilling the Central Purpose of Your Life* (Nashville: Thomas Nelson, 2003), 31ff.
22. Ibid., 32.

23. Dorothy Sayers, "Why Work?" in Mark R. Schwehn and Dorothy C. Bass, eds., *Leading Lives That Matter: What We Should Do and Who We Should Be* (Grand Rapids, MI: Eerdmans, 2006), 195.
24. Os Guiness, *The Call: Finding and Fulfilling the Central Purpose of Your Life* (Nashville: Thomas Nelson, 2003), 50.
25. Mother Teresa, as quoted in Les and Leslie Parrot, *The One Year Love Talk Devotional for Couples* (Carol Stream, IL: Tyndale, 2011), Jan. 3.

EIGHT. WEAVER OF DREAMS

26. Charles Spurgeon, *Spurgeon's Sermons on Prayer* (Peabody, MA: Hendrickson Pub., 2007), 163.